The Compassionate Kitchen

ALSO BY THUBTEN CHODRON

Approaching the Buddhist Path
(with the Dalai Lama)

Buddhism: One Teacher, Many Traditions
(with the Dalai Lama)

Buddhism for Beginners

Choosing Simplicity (ed.)

Cultivating a Compassionate Heart

Don't Believe Everything You Think

The Foundation of Buddhist Practice
(with the Dalai Lama)

Good Karma

How to Free Your Mind

An Open-Hearted Life
(with Dr. Russell Kolts)

Open Heart, Clear Mind

Practical Ethics and Profound Emptiness (ed.)

Taming the Mind

Transforming Adversity into Joy and Courage (ed.)

Working with Anger

THE

Compassionate Kitchen

*Buddhist Practices for Eating with
Mindfulness and Gratitude*

THUBTEN CHODRON

SHAMBHALA
Boulder · 2018

Shambhala Publications, Inc.
4720 Walnut Street
Boulder, Colorado 80301
www.shambhala.com

9 8 7 6 5 4 3 2 1

FIRST EDITION
Printed in the United States of America

⊗ This edition is printed on acid-free paper that meets the
American National Standards Institute z39.48 Standard.
♻ This book is printed on 30% postconsumer recycled paper.
For more information please visit www.shambhala.com.

Shambhala Publications is distributed worldwide by Penguin Random
House, Inc., and its subsidiaries.

Designed by Steve Dyer

LIBRARY OF CONGRESS CATALOGING-IN-PUBLICATION DATA
Names: Thubten Chodron, 1950– author.
Title: The compassionate kitchen: Buddhist practices for eating with
mindfulness and gratitude / Bhiksuni Thubten Chodron.
Description: First Edition. | Boulder: Shambhala, 2018. | Includes
bibliographical references.
Identifiers: LCCN 2018002243 | ISBN 9781611806342 (pbk.: alk. paper)
Subjects: LCSH: Food—Religious aspects—Buddhism.
Classification: LCC BQ4570.F6 T48 2018 | DDC 294.3/4446—dc23
LC record available at https://lccn.loc.gov/2018002243

CONTENTS

PREFACE

F OOD NOURISHES our body and is indispensable for good health. Likewise, reflection and meditation nourish us spiritually. Along with receiving teachings and offering service to others, reflecting on the Dharma is essential for our spiritual health. This book is about combining spiritual and physical nourishment to create healthy, happy, and peaceful lives.

A Brief Introduction to Buddhism

Since some readers may be new to Buddhism, a brief introduction is in line. Buddhism began with the awakening of Shakyamuni Buddha in India approximately twenty-five centuries ago. It is based on the idea that all sentient beings (*sattvas*) want happiness, not suffering, but our approach to creating the causes for happiness is mistaken and so we often wind up experiencing unsatisfactory conditions instead. Each of us sentient beings has great potential—our Buddha nature—to make our lives meaningful and to bring about happiness for ourselves and others, but we are largely unaware of this hidden treasure inside our minds.

The basic framework of Buddhism centers on the four truths: unsatisfactory conditions (*duhkha*), their origin, their cessation, and the path to the cessation of all unsatisfactory conditions. Unsatisfactory conditions include aging, sickness, death, being separated from what is dear to us, not getting what we want, and disappointment in the long term even when things go the way we want in the short term. The origins of this situation lie principally in our own minds: they are the "three poisons" of ignorance that misapprehends the nature of reality; clinging attachment that is greedy and self-centered; and anger that wants to harm those who cause us harm or interfere with our happiness.

Since ignorance is erroneous, it can be counteracted by the wisdom that correctly realizes reality. Cultivating this wisdom is the core of the path, but other emotions and views need to be cultivated as well, such as ethical conduct that abandons harming others, the determination to be free from the cycle of constantly recurring problems called cyclic existence, love that wishes all sentient beings to have happiness and its causes, compassion that wishes them to be free of suffering and its causes, and meditative concentration that can focus one-pointedly on virtuous objects. Bringing about this internal transformation in our minds and hearts requires learning, reflection, meditation, and, of course, practice and time.

The Buddhist path is open for everyone to follow. Most Buddhists are lay practitioners—people with families and jobs—but some choose to become monastics who take more ethical precepts and devote their lives to the Dharma, the Buddha's teachings. Many monastics live in monasteries—Sravasti Abbey is one of them—where we not only study, practice, and teach the Dharma but also serve society. We invite guests to come and practice with us.

How This Book Came About

I have been a Buddhist nun since 1977 and have eaten literally tons of food since then. In those years, I have lived in a variety of situations — sometimes residing in Dharma centers, at times staying with families or living alone, and at other times abiding in a monastery. In all these settings, one constant practice has been a brief contemplation before eating and the recitation of verses that transform my attitude toward eating.

Sravasti Abbey, where I've lived since 2003, is a monastery in eastern Washington State. It is home to a residential monastic community as well as lay trainees. We hold many events, courses, and retreats in which we are joined by guests from all over the world. Of course, we all eat together. One of the first things guests learn is our contemplation before meals and the offering of food. Almost everyone comments that this practice slows them down and makes them more mindful of why and how they eat. It also increases their awareness of the kindness of others as well as the numerous causes and conditions that must come together for a meal to occur. Many retreatants and guests have brought the practice of offering their food back to their homes and found that it changed the quality of their families' mealtimes.

Our life at the Abbey is based on communal values, all of which in one way or another can be related to food. We cherish the environment and the beings we share it with, and we work to counteract consumerism, pollution, and waste. Gender equality is important to us, as are ethical conduct and generosity. Consideration of and respect for others are essential, and we value nonharmfulness, gratitude, humility, rejoicing at others' success and happiness, making amends for our misdeeds, and practicing forgiveness. Our most important value is compassion. Articulating these values, I could write a chapter about each one and how it relates to food. If you are so inclined, pause for a minute and think about this, making examples of how to implement these values in your consumption of food.

At the request of Abbey residents and guests, in May and June of 2016, I gave a series of talks about nourishing our minds while nourishing our bodies. These talks were given just before lunch, like all our Bodhisattva's Breakfast Corner (BBC) talks. (Years ago, the talks were given before breakfast. We later moved them to just before lunch, but the original title remains.) The talks were transcribed and edited and additional material was added to form this book. You can listen to the original talks online at https://thubtenchodron .org/series/buddha-at-my-table/.

While these talks were given in the context of how we procure and prepare food, offer and eat it, conclude the meal, and clean up afterward in a monastic community, they cover many aspects that apply to family life as well. My hope is that lay practitioners will adapt the contents of this book to your own needs, depending on your family's circumstances and the ages of your children. I also believe that you will find it interesting to learn a little about monastic life; it will enrich your appreciation of the Three Jewels: the Buddha, Dharma, and Sangha.

There is so much to say about Buddhism and food; this slim volume does not purport to cover it all. I encourage you to do more research and inquiry, as well as put into practice what you have learned so that it benefits your own and others' lives.

Our friend, Gen Heywood, a professional photographer, took photos of all the activities related to food at the Abbey, from donors shopping to offering the food and cleaning up after meals. You can see them at https://thubtenchodron.org/books/compassionate-kitchen/.

Overview

This volume begins with a brief discussion of the Sangha's (monastic community) relationship with food at the time of the Buddha. The Buddha wanted everyone to learn and practice the liberating path he taught. In that regard he established and taught the fourfold assembly of fully ordained men and women and male and female lay practitioners. He set up a heart connection between the monastics and lay followers that exists to this day. Chapter 1 describes how this is practiced in a modern-day monastery.

Since our intention is the most important aspect of any action we do, chapter 2 discusses our motivation for eating and explains the five contemplations from the Chinese Buddhist tradition. These are recited before the main meal—which in our case is lunch—and contemplated during all meals.

Chapter 3 describes the actual offering of the meal, especially consecrating the food, paying homage to the Three Jewels, and then offering the food to them. We do a longer offering at lunchtime and an abbreviated one at other meals or when having a snack.

Chapter 4 discusses food in a family setting, especially how to introduce children to mindful eating and to making offerings. All of us, whether lay or monastic, practice maintaining mindfulness and a positive motivation while eating. This is discussed in chapter 5, while chapter 6 goes into the topic of what to eat. Following this, in chapter 7, we learn about how to conclude the main meal—offering leftovers to the hungry ghosts, purifying any faults we may have accrued, and dedicating the merit for the benefactors and all sentient beings.

Chapter 8 concerns working with attachment to food and chapter 9 with Buddhist precepts and customs regarding food. Chapter 10 brings in stories from two of the Abbey's supporters who practice the Dharma at home with their families. Both have had an unhealthy relationship with food in the past and share with us how learning and practicing the Buddha's teachings has helped them arrive at a balanced attitude. The last piece in chapter 10, by one of the Abbey's nuns who is also a nurse practitioner, discusses health concerns regarding food.

Please refer to the glossary, which will help you understand the meaning of unfamiliar terms.

Appreciation

I first pay homage to the Buddha, who, with great compassion, taught the liberating path to awakening, and to the lineage of practitioners who for twenty-five centuries have practiced and preserved these precious teachings. I pay sincere respect to my personal teachers, especially His Holiness the Dalai Lama, Tsenzhap Serkong Rinpoche, and Kyabje

Zopa Rinpoche, who have patiently taught and guided me for many years.

Many people helped with the production of this book. Volunteers videoed and transcribed these talks. Ven. Tenzin Tsepal did the initial editing. All mistakes are my own.

These timeless teachings show us how to make the most of our lives by transforming the daily activity of eating into extensive causes for full awakening. I hope you will benefit from them. Bon appétit and peaceful heart!

BHIKSUNI THUBTEN CHODRON
Sravasti Abbey, 2018

The Compassionate Kitchen

1

Eating as Spiritual Practice

An Introduction to Food at Sravasti Abbey

A N INTRODUCTION to how food fits into our spiritual practice at Sravasti Abbey will help to set the stage. It may startle you to learn that we don't buy any of our food and eat only what is offered to us. Rather than catering to our preoccupation and enthusiasm for food and drink, we are encouraged to cultivate an honest and beneficial relationship with our daily bread, nourishing the seeds of our simplified way of life and our altruistic aspirations. We are vegetarian, and although we eat to sustain our lives so we can engage in spiritual practice and benefit others, I must confess that sweets sneak onto the buffet table from time to time.

Everything we eat is visible to others. We fill our bowls with food on the buffet table that has been offered for community consumption. Equality in sharing resources is important for community harmony, so snacks that everyone can have are placed on a special counter. According to Vinaya—the monastic discipline established by the Buddha—we cannot go into the kitchen, where food offered to the entire community is kept, to serve ourselves or to raid the refrigerator.

There are no private stashes of chocolate, energy bars, and so forth in our rooms.

Having a predictable daily schedule helps us to regulate our appetites: breakfast, lunch, and medicine meal are served at 7:30 a.m., 12:00 p.m., and 6:00 p.m. The meals are simple, avoiding complicated and time-consuming recipes and allowing us to appreciate the natural goodness of fruits, vegetables, grains, and beans. Helping with the preparation, cooking, and cleanup adds to our contentment and the gratitude that we have for our food and all the people involved in growing, transporting, offering, and preparing it. Chanting while receiving and offering the food and dedicating the merit for all our supporters brings us into the present moment with gratitude. Normally we eat the first part of our meal in silence, which enables us to enjoy our meal with a calm, unhurried mental state. During retreats, the entire meal is usually eaten in silence, giving us the chance to spend time alone with our own thoughts and to connect with others in the peaceful medium of silence.

Although some of this may seem extreme ("You don't buy food?! Won't you starve?!") or downright impossible ("How can I eat in silence when I'm feeding a toddler and my infant starts to wail?"), keep an open, playful mind and see what fits you and your situation, and what you could adapt so that it works for you.

An Economy of Generosity: The Heart Connection between Monastics and Lay Followers

At the time of the Buddha, the various groups of renunciates in India lived a simple lifestyle. A significant part of that involved going on alms round in the villages, where families who respected the renunciates' spiritual goals and practice offered them food. As this was the socially accepted custom, the Buddha lived likewise. After his awakening, when disciples gathered around him, the Sangha — the community of monastics — arose, and the Buddha stipulated that they, too, would go on alms round.

Alms round, or *pindapat*, is not begging. The Sangha did not ask for food; they silently stood in front of a house with their alms bowls. If families wished to offer food, they would put it in the bowls. If they did not, after a minute or two, the monastics would go to the next house and do the same.

Once the populace saw the qualities of the Buddha's Sangha, those with means began to invite these monastics into their homes for meals. After the meal, one of the Sangha members would give a teaching. It was a beautiful interchange based on an economy of generosity, with lay followers offering food that nourishes the body and the Sangha offering the Dharma that nourishes the heart and mind. In this way, a relationship of interdependence between the Sangha and the lay community arose. Everybody benefited not only from receiving from the other but also, and especially, from cultivating a motivation of benevolence and care when making their respective offering.

The Sangha wandered from one village to another; they settled in one place only during the three months of *varsa* — the retreat during the monsoon months. At that time, wealthy donors would offer accommodation and food and the Sangha would dwell in *viharas* — simple buildings offered by the benefactors, often in a park. After the Buddha's passing, the Sangha began to establish communities and later monasteries. Lay followers would bring food to the monasteries, and the Sangha would teach them the Dharma and encourage them to live by the five lay precepts.[1] Twice a month, on new- and full-moon days, lay followers went to the monasteries to receive the eight precepts, which they kept for one day.[2] On that day, they practiced the Dharma together with the Sangha.

When Buddhism spread through South and Southeast Asia, the climate and culture were conducive for maintaining the tradition of going on alms round. In China and Tibet this was not the case, and so the Sangha's way of procuring food changed. In Chinese Chan (Zen) monasteries they often grew their food, and in China and Tibet lay followers would bring groceries or cooked food to monasteries to offer to the Sangha. In modern-day America, going on alms round would present interesting challenges. Some of our friends at a Zen monastery wanted to go on alms round in their local town, and the town council required them to get a parade permit to do it!

In establishing Sravasti Abbey, I wanted to duplicate the interdependent relationship between the Sangha and the lay community but in a more modern context that is convenient for our supporters. The Abbey is twenty minutes' drive from our one-stoplight town of Newport, WA, and about an hour and a quarter to the closest cities of Spokane and Coeur d'Alene. Going on alms round would not work, and having lay followers bring cooked food to the monastery every day would be asking too much of supporters who were busy with family and work. So I resolved that we would eat only the food that was offered to us, although we would store it and prepare it ourselves.

When I first mentioned this to others, people protested, "But you're going to starve!" It's true, there are hardly any Buddhists in the area (the Abbey is in a conservative, rural area), but I wanted to try it anyway. The day the original residents of the Abbey—two cats and I—moved in, the few local Buddhists had filled the fridge and cupboards with food. They later organized among themselves to bring food weekly, which I appreciated greatly. Only on one occasion was the fridge empty (there was still canned food in the cupboards), and that was only for a day or two. We haven't starved and instead have been the recipients of tremendous generosity that we do our best to repay through our practice and teaching.

A few months after I moved to the Abbey, someone at the *Spokesman-Review*, the main newspaper in Spokane, called and asked to do an article about the Abbey. During the interview, she asked how we maintained ourselves. I responded that we were supported solely by donations and told her about eating only the food others had offered. She mentioned this in the article, and a day or two later a person we had never met arrived at the Abbey with an SUV completely full of food. We were speechless.

We have many courses and retreats open to the public. On our website and when people register for events, we explain that everyone here eats only the food that is offered. The retreatants and guests bring food to offer to the Sangha, and the Sangha then shares it with everyone who visits us, no matter how long they stay. Due to people's generosity, we've always had enough to feed thirty to fifty-five people for at least four days. Occasionally we have surplus, which we offer to either the local food bank or to Youth Emergency Services of Pend Oreille County, a nonprofit supporting homeless teenagers, where two Abbey monastics serve on the board of directors.

Some of our friends who live far away also want to offer food to the Abbey. The local Buddhists have arranged for them to send funds that the locals then use to purchase food, which they bring to the Abbey. They usually call or email us once a week to say they would like to make a food offering and ask what would be helpful. For years now, they have faithfully made weekly food offerings, even during winter snowstorms and roasting summer days. Other people send us care packages with dry goods or home-baked goods. People's generosity is astounding.

Feeling their kindness, we want to reciprocate. The Abbey does not charge for anything—room, board, or teachings. Dharma books are given freely, with a donation basket nearby. We have an online education program—Sravasti Abbey Friends Education (SAFE)—as well as thousands of teachings on YouTube and two websites full of Dharma materials. All of this is freely offered. We want to be generous, too.

To reinforce this economy of generosity, I wrote verses that people recite when they offer groceries to the Abbey. Everyone—guests and monastics alike—gathers around a large alms bowl that contains a portion of the food that is offered. The guests then recite the verse of offering; it is not uncommon for them to choke up and hold back tears while they are reading it:

> With a mind that takes delight in giving, I offer these requisites to the Sangha and the community. Through my offering may they have the food they need to sustain their Dharma practice. They are genuine Dharma

friends who encourage, support, and inspire me along the path. May they become realized practitioners and skilled teachers who will guide us on the path. I rejoice at creating great merit by offering to those intent on virtue, and dedicate this for the awakening of all sentient beings. Through my generosity, may we all have conducive circumstances to develop heartfelt love, compassion, and altruism for each other, and to realize the ultimate nature of reality.

The Sangha then replies:

Your generosity is inspiring, and we are humbled by your faith in the Three Jewels. We will endeavor to keep our precepts as best as we can, to live simply, to cultivate equanimity, love, compassion, and joy, and to realize the ultimate nature so that we can repay your kindness in sustaining our lives. Although we are not perfect, we will do our best to be worthy of your offering. Together we will create peace in a chaotic world.

This reply emphasizes that by working together monastics and lay followers aim to create peace in a chaotic world. As the Sangha recites this verse, we are reminded that we have food to eat due to the kindness of other people who work hard and then choose, out of the goodness of their hearts, to share their food with us. To repay their kindness in sustaining our lives, we must hold our precepts and uphold the Dharma as best as we can. To be worthy of their faith and generosity, we must study, contemplate, and meditate, and also share the Dharma with others.

We gently remind the lay people that we are not perfect, because sometimes people think that anyone wearing robes must be near Buddhahood and will never make mistakes. We are not perfect, but we are very committed to working on our minds and holding our ethical precepts as best as we can.

In this brief exchange when food is respectfully offered and gratefully received, we remember our interdependent nature. Because everyone—monastics and lay followers—has a wholesome motivation and a generous heart, we all create merit. This is very different from someone bringing food and tossing it on the counter, saying, "Here you go." Families can adapt this ritual. As a child, I would have been more aware of my parents' kindness and hard work had we done a simple exchange like this. Instead, I selfishly expected food to be there and complained when it wasn't what I liked.

The local supporters made another request: "We want to make sure our mind has a Dharma motivation when we go shopping for the groceries. Please write a verse that we can recite and contemplate before going into the store." So I wrote the following verse:

> Offering food sustains the lives of others. I delight in providing physical nourishment to the Sangha, knowing that their practice and the teachings they give as a result of it will nourish my heart and the hearts of many others. I will have a calm heart and mind while mindfully selecting appropriate items to offer, and will have a deep sense of satisfaction knowing that the Sangha appreciates this offering. We have a heart connection, and together we will create peace in a chaotic world.

Our volunteers have reported that pausing and contemplating this verse has helped them to think about the import of what they were doing, instead of simply rushing through the grocery store in order to check it off their to-do list. The words emphasize cultivating a good motivation and being aware of the positive results our actions will have on others and on ourselves. That is how we've organized the offering and receiving of food at the Abbey since its inception in 2003.

Inside the Abbey's Kitchen

The practice of going on alms round in the Buddha's time meant that monastics could not prepare or ask for the food they liked. We are to eat whatever we receive with gratitude. To do this, we have to work with our attachment to certain foods and shift our attention from liking or disliking the taste and texture of particular foods to awareness of the kindness of others for sustaining our lives.

Not preparing food also prevented monastics from killing worms in fruit and vegetables when washing or cooking them. The Buddha did not consider plants to be sentient beings: even though they are biologically alive, they lack consciousness. However, the Jains considered plants to be sentient. So that people would not criticize the Buddha's monastics unnecessarily for harming living beings by cooking vegetables that may contain insects, the Buddha asked lay followers to prepare and cook the meals.

Nowadays, reducing attachment to favorite foods is a necessary and important practice, but inadvertently killing worms and other insects while preparing the food is not a big concern as most store-bought produce does not have these.

However, when people offer us fruits and vegetables that were grown in their family gardens, we look out for insects and take care not to harm them.

Unlike in ancient India, women as well as men are now in the workforce. The Abbey's supporters cannot take time off of work to drive over an hour to the Abbey, prepare a meal for a number of people, and then drive back to their workplace in the city. Being sensitive to the needs of lay supporters, as the Buddha himself was, we decided that we would prepare our food. This has another practical component as well: the state requires cooks at the Abbey to have a food preparation license. Monastics take the test for this license, so they become the head cooks, while guests assist in chopping vegetables and other tasks.

To help us cultivate detachment, we practice eating whatever is served. While our meals are simple, they offer enough variety so everyone can find something to eat. We prepare side dishes for those who require gluten-free or dairy-free diets. On days that the menu isn't exactly what we prefer, we practice eating what is offered with gratitude, remembering that many people on this planet lack even food for subsistence. To be honest, that doesn't mean nobody complains. However, complaints are not indulged and people are reminded of the verse we recite before eating, "By seeing this food as medicine, I will consume it without attachment or complaint." I encourage people to remember our motivation: "We are here to train our mind, tune in to our Buddha nature, and create peace in a chaotic world."

Monastics take turns cooking. Each morning the community has a fifteen- to twenty-minute stand-up meeting where we share how we will offer service that day. To help us set our motivation for the ensuing activities — be they cooking, working in the forest, transcribing teachings, or preparing Dharma talks — we recite the following verse together:

> We are grateful for the opportunity to offer service to the Buddha, Dharma, and Sangha, and to sentient beings. While working with others, differences in ideas and ways of doing things may arise. These are natural and are a source of creative exchange; our minds don't need to make them into conflicts. We will endeavor to listen deeply and communicate wisely and kindly as we work together for our common goal. By using our body and speech to support the values we deeply believe in — generosity, kindness, ethical conduct, love, and compassion — we will create great merit, which we dedicate for the awakening of all beings.

In a family setting, this verse could be adapted and recited by the whole family before each family member embarks on doing his or her chores. Seeing chores as "offering service" rather than "work" changes our attitude and our mood. When parents and children recite this verse together, they remember that everyone participates and contributes to the well-being of the family. Friends of the Abbey have brought this verse into their workplace, and even to office meetings.

Before beginning to prepare the meal, the cooks for that day gather together in the kitchen and recite and contemplate this verse:

We will offer service by preparing a meal for the community of Dharma practitioners. We are fortunate to have the opportunity to prepare and cook this food. The food will nourish their bodies and the love we put into preparing it will nourish their hearts. Preparing food is an expression of our kind heart. When we chop, mix, and cook, we will work with mindfulness and a relaxed mind. We will leave aside idle talk, and speak with gentle and low voices. The menu will be simple and healthy, free from the distraction of elaborate and complicated menus. We will wash the veggies and fruits well, thinking that we are cleansing defilements from the minds of sentient beings with the nectar of wisdom. Out of consideration for those who will clean up after the meal, we will tidy up after ourselves. Let's take joy in working harmoniously together for the benefit of all!

This verse, too, can be said in a family. It transforms our motivation from "I *have to* cook (sigh)" to "I have the opportunity to be of benefit to others." It also gives children a way to join in food preparation and to be in contact with fresh food, rather than fast food.

At lunchtime, the bell at the Abbey is rung and the conch blown to call everyone to the dining room. Before eating, we have a short Dharma talk. We post this on the Abbey's YouTube channel later in the day to share with others. You can watch these BBC talks and more at youtube.com /sravastiabbey. The playlist of the latest BBC (Bodhisattva's Breakfast Corner) talks is at https://www.youtube.com/user /sravastiabbey/playlists?view=1&sort=dd.

2

The Taste of Altruism
Our Motivation for Eating

As DHARMA PRACTITIONERS, we aspire to imbue all our daily actions with a positive motivation — one of kindness that understands our interdependent nature. Even more important than the specific action we do is the reason why we do it. The motivation we bring to each action impacts its results, and eating is no exception. By cultivating our motivation for eating and by remembering our long- and short-term purposes, we can transform otherwise ordinary actions such as eating.

We can approach eating with various motivations. Very often we eat to enjoy the taste of the food. Here attachment to sense pleasure and greed for what gives us this pleasure easily arise. Attachment is considered an afflictive mental state because it is based on exaggerating the good qualities of something or someone and then clinging to it. Attachment makes our mind very narrow and self-centered; a mind filled with craving has no room for generosity. Thus actions motivated by clinging attachment become nonvirtuous and, in the long term, lead to suffering.

It is important to understand that there is nothing wrong

with experiencing pleasure. The path to awakening does not involve tortuous self-denial and asceticism; the Buddha opposed such activity. Pleasure is not a problem. We run into trouble when we become attached to the pleasure and to people and things that bring it. It's the attachment, not the pleasure itself, that leads us to lie to get what we want, to steal others' property, or to kill to protect our possessions or honor. So the trick is to experience the pleasure without clinging to it, being depressed when it's gone, or trying to recreate it later. As my teacher Lama Thubten Yeshe used to tell us, "Comes, comes. Goes, goes. Don't cling."

We could also eat to nourish our body and sustain our life. If we do this in a balanced way without greedily seeking more and better, our motivation is karmically neutral, bringing neither pleasant nor painful results.

On the basis of such a neutral motivation, we can cultivate a virtuous motivation by expanding our perspective. For example, we think that we eat to keep our body healthy and to renew our physical strength so that we can practice the Dharma—that is, so that we can abandon harmful actions, words, and thoughts and transform our mind into excellent qualities such as love, compassion, and wisdom. By doing so we will create the causes to attain a fortunate rebirth, such as a precious human life with all the necessary conditions to progress on the path. This is a virtuous motivation; it is more expansive than seeking only our immediate pleasure, yet it is still narrow because we're concerned with only our own future rebirths. If we expand our intention further, we can develop the motivation to practice the Dharma in order to attain liberation from the constantly recurring problems of cyclic existence. This will bring a better result. And if we enhance our motivation even further, we can generate *bodhicitta* — that is, we will seek to become a fully awakened Buddha in order to benefit others and lead them on the path to awakening. This is the most noble motivation, and any action — even cooking, eating, or doing the dishes — done with this intention will contribute to our attaining Buddhahood one day.

Thought for Food: The Five Contemplations

At the Abbey, lunch is our main meal, so we spend more time than at other meals contemplating our motivation for eating. We do this by reciting the five contemplations, which are from the Chinese Buddhist tradition. The five contemplations are as follows:

1. I contemplate all the causes and conditions and the kindness of others by which I have received this food.
2. I contemplate my own practice, constantly trying to improve it.
3. I contemplate my mind, cautiously guarding it from wrongdoing, greed, and other defilements.
4. I contemplate this food, treating it as wondrous medicine to nourish my body.
5. I contemplate the aim of Buddhahood, accepting and consuming this food in order to accomplish it.

We pause after reciting each of the five contemplations so that we can reflect on its meaning.

   1. *I contemplate all the causes and conditions and the kindness of others by which I have received this food.*

The first contemplation encourages us to reflect on all the causes and conditions that have come together for us to receive the food. The original version in Chinese doesn't include the phrase "the kindness of others." I added that phrase, because when we reflect on the causes and conditions of our meal, it becomes obvious that it came about due to the kindness and efforts of others. That phrase explicitly reminds us that having received kindness, we want to repay it by paying it forward.

Our meal has many causes and conditions. Some are physical: the seeds that grew into the grains, fruits, and vegetables. Some are karmic: our practice of generosity either earlier in this life or in previous lives when we offered funds to purchase food or gave food directly to others. Recalling this motivates us to continue being generous by giving food to others now. Helping others is a way of helping ourselves just as harming others is a way of harming ourselves.

While this sounds easy to do, it involves confronting our miserliness. When we are hungry, do we serve others first and distribute portions equally? When we have limited funds, do we share the little food we have with the homeless people we pass on the streets? Do we share the food we like with friends—or do we share the food we don't like, in the hopes that they might like it? When we offer fruit or baked goods to the Three Jewels, do we put the best on the altar, or do we offer the bruised fruit and day-old baked goods and keep the best for ourselves? It is important to recognize our miserliness and ask ourselves if it creates the causes and conditions to receive food in the future or if it impedes it. While miserliness may give us some immediate benefit, it isn't conducive to our becoming the kind of person we want to be and it inhibits our spiritual growth.

Awareness of karma and its effects also inspires us to reflect on whether we are creating the causes to have food in future lives. We need to think deeply about that, because our present actions cause our future experiences.

In developed countries we tend to take the presence of food in our kitchens and on our tables for granted. However, having food depends on many causes and conditions that ripen in this lifetime: the climate needs to be good so that crops grow properly, farmers need to be healthy so that they can plant and tend to the crops, the infrastructure in the country must be adequate to transport the food, and the country must be peaceful so that the food can reach the residents. We see so vividly in war-torn countries that crops cannot grow and emergency food supplies are often unable to reach people because of the fighting.

The kindness and efforts of others also enable us to be well nourished. Other people grow our food. Unlike in ancient times when every family had a garden, nowadays very few people grow all the food they consume. Other people plant, water, fertilize, harvest, sort, process, package, transport, stock, and sell the food we eat. In many countries, animals till the ground and carry the harvests on their backs. Having all the ingredients to prepare just one meal is dependent on countless other living beings.

At the Abbey we do not eat meat. For those of you who do eat meat, please think of the kindness of other beings who have involuntarily given their bodies and lives for your breakfast, lunch, or dinner. Use that awareness to develop a strong sense of gratitude toward those beings. In future times when you are a high bodhisattva, you will be happy to offer your body for someone else's lunch, but right now you are probably not ready to do that. So at least recite the mantra OM AHBIRAKAY TSARA HUM seven times over the meat to help the sentient beings whose flesh you eat to be reborn in a fortunate realm. You could also resolve to benefit those sentient beings when you attain Dharma realizations in order to repay their kindness in sacrificing their bodies and lives for your meal.

We now have the opportunity to create merit by offering food to the Three Jewels. Just having the chance to do this comes from the kindness of others who have worked so hard in the long chain of activities that brought the food to our table. Our lives, including our ability to practice the Dharma and create merit, are intricately dependent on so many sentient beings. Reflecting in this way is part of the method side of the path, which helps us to generate bodhicitta — the wish to become a fully awakened Buddha, in order to most effectively benefit all sentient beings.

On the wisdom side of the path, we investigate how things are produced by causes and conditions and therefore do not exist inherently. They do not have their own essence, and they exist only because their causes existed. The mere fact that the existence of things depends on other things — their causes, conditions, and their parts, for example — shows that they cannot be independent. They can't possibly have their own inherent or independent essence. In just the first contemplation of the causes and conditions and the kindness of others by which we have received this food, we practice both the method and wisdom sides of the path to awakening.

2. *I contemplate my own practice, constantly trying to improve it.*

The original Chinese version of this line is roughly translated as "I contemplate my own practice, to ensure I am worthy of this food." This calls us to reflect on whether we are keeping our precepts and practicing properly, such that we are worthy of the generosity of others who give food with faith in the Sangha. I changed the wording because talking about "being worthy of having food" can make some people uncomfortable. They may begin to feel guilty and disparage themselves, which is not at all useful and is certainly not the intended outcome of this contemplation. Rather, we want to remember that people have offered us food out of the goodness of their hearts. They worked hard to earn the money to purchase it, and we would lack integrity if we took their kindness for granted. Especially when people with faith offer food to the Sangha, we have the responsibility to improve our practice and keep our precepts well to uphold our part of the relationship.

The Buddha described four types of practitioners who receive the offerings of requisites—food, clothing, shelter, and medicine—from those with faith. The first group, those who don't keep precepts well yet consume offerings, are like thieves, taking what is not rightfully theirs. The second group consists of those who don't have any realizations but guard their precepts and diligently work to improve. They are like debtors taking out a loan of food that can nourish them so that they can continue to practice and gain realizations of the path. The third group is practitioners who are stream-enterers, once-returners, and non-returners. They have realized the nature of reality but must continue to meditate on it in order to purify their minds of all afflictions. They resemble people who partake of their inheritance. It is not theirs yet, but because these practitioners are *aryas*—those who have realized emptiness directly—their final goal of liberation or Buddhahood is in sight. Thus they are accepting what will soon be theirs. The fourth group consists of *arhats*—liberated beings—bodhisattvas on the eighth ground and above, and Buddhas. They are the rightful owners. Because they have eliminated the afflictive obscurations, they are completely worthy to receive and enjoy the offerings of food and other requisites.

This contemplation helps us to understand that we have an obligation related to our choice to become monastics. We should not be proud, thinking, "I hold precepts so others should give me food." As my teacher Lama Thubten Yeshe used to say, "Your mantra should be 'I am the servant of others.' You must always remind yourselves of this." We are like debtors taking a loan of food so that we can practice well now, gain realizations, and repay others' kindness by teaching them the Dharma and leading them on the path to awakening.

> 3. *I contemplate my mind, cautiously guarding it from wrongdoing, greed, and other defilements.*

Each of the monastics at Sravasti Abbey has an alms bowl that she or he uses to eat. We go through the buffet line in ordination order, taking enough to nourish our bodies but not excess. From the moment we begin to fill our bowls, we want to have an attitude that guards against any wrongdoing, such as greed and complaining.

Wrongdoing may take many forms. If twenty people are

present for lunch and twenty spring rolls are set out for the meal, taking two of them for ourselves would be greedy and inconsiderate. If we're in the front of the line, taking huge portions of our favorite dishes so that there is not enough for the people later in the line is also negligent. If food remains after everyone has taken some, we can go back for seconds.

The greedy mind is insatiable. No matter how much we have or receive, the craving mind wants more. This greedy mind is also sneaky. We may take a moderate portion but then check out others' bowls to see if they took more than we did. Or we may eat quickly so we can go back for seconds before others do. This is one reason we have a precept not to look in other people's bowls; how much food our neighbor takes is not our business. How much *we* take is our business, and we must make sure not to pile so much in our bowl that other people don't have a chance to receive their share.

In any situation where the Sangha is given offerings, we should not take the offered item twice, even if somebody thinks we didn't receive it and offers it to us again. If that happens, we should indicate that we have already received the offering to ensure that everybody receives it equally. If someone offers socks to everyone in the community, any extras are put in the storage area. When someone needs another pair of socks, he or she asks the store manager.

When monastics attend teachings with His Holiness the Dalai Lama in India, a small monetary offering is often distributed to all the Sangha members who are present. Sometimes two monks come by at different times to distribute the rupee note, and we could easily take the offering a second time without anyone noticing. However, accepting a second offering would constitute stealing. Since we are working hard to purify our minds, adding more pollution to it for the sake of money makes no sense.

Another defilement to guard against is a restless, complaining attitude. We may think, "I wish they put more salt in this food" or "They shouldn't put so much salt in the food." The mind complains, "I don't like this food. I wish they would make something I like" or "I need more protein," "I need more carbs," "I need more sugar. What's wrong with sugar anyway?" Our mantra becomes "I need, I need, I need." Do we really need this? Or do we crave it? Are we seeking happiness in external objects, even though we have what is necessary to keep our body healthy? When this complaining, insatiable mind of greed arises, we must remember that we are monastics and that our job is to accept with gratitude whatever is offered to us. Personally speaking, some days there's not much that accords with my taste or the way my digestive system works. But part of my practice is to accept what is offered and be content with that.

One of the criteria for practitioners who want to cultivate serenity and concentration is contentment. If we lack this quality, we may meditate for a long time in a secluded place, but our concentration will not deepen because our mind will constantly daydream about everything we crave.

Of course, if you're not able to eat certain foods and feel sick after eating a particular food, you can politely mention it to the kitchen manager. At the Abbey, people who require a gluten-free or dairy-free diet can say so. People who cannot eat beans or tomatoes can mention that, too. Then the cook can consider changing the menu or preparing an alternative dish. But some days the cook may put out a cake offered by a supporter, with no gluten-free alternative. That is the time to practice fortitude. Realize that contrary to what the dissatisfied, greedy mind says, you will survive without dessert. In fact, tomorrow you won't even remember that you didn't have dessert today. It is difficult indeed to satisfy a mind with craving, and we'll be much happier if we cultivate contentment and gratitude. These qualities make us free; craving and dissatisfaction imprison us.

4. *I contemplate this food, treating it as wondrous medicine to nourish my body.*

It's important to remember that we don't eat just for pleasure. The main reason we eat is to nourish our bodies, not to look attractive or strong or to develop an impressive physical appearance. We eat to sustain our lives and maintain our physical health; food is a wondrous medicine that does this.

His Holiness the Dalai Lama often says that while everyone wants to live long, praying for a long life makes sense only if we use our lives to create virtue, purify our minds, and progress along the path to full awakening. Praying to have a long life in order to create nonvirtue doesn't help us at all.

If we are sincere about maintaining our lives and health, we should take the "medicine" properly by eating a healthy, balanced diet. This may mean changing our eating habits. We may like eating a lot of salt, sugar, and oil, but they are not wondrous medicines that nourish our bodies. Rather, they destroy our health by contributing to high blood pressure, obesity, diabetes, and other illnesses.

Food conglomerates have done numerous tests to discover what flavors people crave, and the ingredients that create them. Oil, salt, and sugar win the prize. In order to make more profit, these companies put large amounts of these three ingredients in processed food and fast food. Although we may like the taste of products made with these three ingredients, when we eat too much of them they become destructive poison, the opposite of wondrous medicine.

As Dharma practitioners, we are aware that a precious human life with all the conditions for Dharma practice is hard to come by. Having attained this life, we have a rare opportunity to make significant progress on the path to awakening. To do that, we want to have a long, healthy life so that we have more time to practice. Since the food we eat plays a powerful role in this, we want to eat properly and maintain a normal weight as best as we can. That means not being too thin and not being overweight, because both of these increase the risk of health problems. Also, we feel better and have more energy when our weight is normal, which is definitely an aid to practice. As monastics, keeping our bodies healthy so that we can practice and serve society makes good use of the offerings we receive.

Personally speaking, I feel much better physically and emotionally when my weight is in the normal range. This also brings a sense of contentment here and now. When we don't listen to our bodies but let craving dictate what we eat and how much we eat, we don't feel good about ourselves. Stuffing ourselves full of cookies, ice cream, sweetened sodas, or potato chips doesn't make us feel content. Physically it makes us feel heavy and sluggish, especially after the sugar high wears off. Mentally, we feel unhappy with ourselves for being unable to withstand craving and allowing it to run our lives.

Actually, food is not the strongest object of craving; craving for reputation, praise, and approval runs much deeper.

The great masters say that overcoming attachment to food is easy compared to subduing attachment to reputation, love, approval, appreciation, and praise. We need to reduce our craving and attachment slowly by seeing their faults and by realizing that the things we crave don't have happiness inside them. The fulfillment and joy gained from spiritual practice and from abandoning craving is much greater.

> 5. *I contemplate the aim of Buddhahood, accepting and consuming this food in order to accomplish it.*

In the previous contemplation, we made the determination to care for our body by seeing food as wondrous medicine. This verse prompts us to contemplate what we will do after nourishing our body. We will hold the Dharma close to our heart and will practice the path and attain full awakening for the benefit of all sentient beings. We seek not only our own liberation from cyclic existence but also the liberation of all sentient beings. To accomplish that, we want to purify our mind completely and develop all our excellent qualities limitlessly. In short, we want to become Buddhas so we'll have the wisdom, compassion, and power necessary to benefit all others most effectively. This is the altruistic intention of bodhicitta. Working toward the noble goal of Buddhahood makes our life highly meaningful.

. . .

Each day when we recite these lines, we remind ourselves of our long-term aims and make a commitment to remain faithful to them. It's essential for monastics to remember that people have offered food to us because they believe in what we're doing as Dharma practitioners. We want to repay their kindness, and the best way to do that is to progress on the path to full awakening for their benefit and to do what we can to benefit society now. We will eat healthy food with mindfulness to have a long life in order to do this.

Lay practitioners remember that so many sentient beings worked very hard to grow, transport, and prepare the food they eat. They want to repay the kindness of those people by practicing the path to full awakening.

By reciting these five contemplations, we remember the short- and long-term purposes for eating our meal. Although it's fine to enjoy tasty food, our long-term purpose is a spiritual one. We don't eat simply for pleasure or to socialize or to become physically attractive. As aspiring bodhisattvas, we again and again dedicate our lives to benefiting sentient beings and to preserving and disseminating the Dharma. While our present aspirations may be fabricated with effort, by continually cultivating them, they will gradually become a part of us and will eventually arise spontaneously.

3

The Main Course
The Actual Offering

HAVING REFLECTED on the five contemplations from the Chinese Buddhist tradition, we now consecrate the food by imagining that it becomes blissful wisdom nectar, pay homage to the Three Jewels, and offer the nectar to them according to verses from the Tibetan Buddhist tradition. Below is the entire set of verses chanted before eating, followed by an explanation of what to think and visualize while chanting each one. You can listen to us chanting the verses at https://thubtenchodron.org/books/compassionate-kitchen/.

OM AH HUM (*repeat three times*)

Great compassionate Protector,
All-knowing Teacher,
Field of merit and good qualities vast as an ocean —
To the Tathagata, I bow.

Through purity, freeing from attachment,
Through virtue, freeing from the lower realms,
Unique, supreme ultimate reality —
To the Dharma that is peace, I bow.

Having freed themselves showing the path to freedom,
  too,
Well established in the trainings.
The holy field endowed with good qualities,
To the Sangha, I bow.

To the supreme teacher, the precious Buddha,
To the supreme refuge, the holy precious Dharma,
To the supreme guides, the precious Sangha,
To all the objects of refuge we make this offering.

May we and all those around us never be separated from
  the Triple Gem in any of our lives.
May we always have the opportunity to make offerings
  to them.
And may we continually receive their blessings and
  inspiration
To progress along the path.

By seeing this food as medicine,
I will consume it without attachment or complaint,
Not to increase my arrogance, strength, or good looks,
But solely to sustain my life.

Transforming Food into Blissful Wisdom Nectar

Before offering our meal to the Three Jewels, we imagine transforming it into something magnificent that is far beyond ordinary food. Imagine that the food is in a beautiful jeweled bowl. It dissolves into emptiness—the absence of inherent existence—and then arises as blissful wisdom nectar.[1] With palms together, chant three times OM AH HUM, which represents the Buddha's body, speech, and mind, and think that the food is purified, transformed into nectar, and becomes inexhaustible.

When you eat, imagine that a small Buddha — who is made of light and embodies the Three Jewels — is at the center of your chest. Offer each mouthful of nectar-like food to him and think that he experiences great bliss. Light radiates from his body and fills your entire body; you feel satisfied and blissful.

A Toast to the Three Jewels: Homage to the Buddha, Dharma, and Sangha

To pay homage to the Three Jewels, visualize Shakyamuni Buddha with a body of golden light in the space in front of you. He is surrounded by numberless Buddhas and bodhisattvas, who are seated as far as the eye can see in the space around him. Next to each Buddha and bodhisattva is a table with Dharma texts on them. The Buddhas are the Buddha Jewel; the Dharma texts represent the Dharma Jewel; and the bodhisattvas are the Sangha Jewel, which also includes all the arhats who have attained liberation from cyclic existence. Don't try to see the Buddhas, bodhisattvas, and texts with your eyes; this is done on a mental level with your imagination. It's the same mental function as imagining your friends when you're not with them.

Here, the important point is to feel that you are in the presence of countless holy beings who have done what you aspire to do — to have an open heart with impartial love and compassion for all living beings. They look at you with complete acceptance and delight because you share their bodhicitta

THE COMPASSIONATE KITCHEN

motivation to benefit sentient beings, and they are happy to guide you on the path to awakening. If you prefer, you can simply visualize Shakyamuni Buddha alone and think that he is the embodiment of all the Buddhas and bodhisattvas.

The analogy of a patient, doctor, medicine, and nurses illustrates how to relate to the Three Jewels. We are the patient: a confused sentient being subject to aging, sickness, and death. Wishing to be healthy, we go to the doctor—the Buddha—who diagnoses our illness and its causes. He tells us that we are suffering from duhkha, the unsatisfactory conditions of cyclic existence. This is caused by ignorance, anger, and clinging attachment. The doctor prescribes the medicine of the Dharma—the teachings describing the path to liberation and awakening. To be well, we must take the medicine. Neglecting to fill the prescription—or filling it, but keeping the medicine on our nightstand without taking it—won't heal us. Similarly, purchasing Dharma books, a Buddha statue, and a *mala* (a Buddhist rosary) won't remove our confusion. We must actually put the Dharma teachings into practice by having a daily meditation practice and applying what we learn to events in our daily life.

Sometimes we forget how to take the medicine or we become confused about what medicine to take at what time. The Sangha are like nurses: by practicing and discussing the Dharma with us, they guide us so that we understand the Dharma and apply it correctly and consistently.

Having taken the medicine according to the instructions, the patient will be cured. Similarly, we will leave cyclic existence behind and enjoy the bliss of liberation.

When paying homage to the Buddha, the Dharma, and the Sangha, chant the following verses and visualize all sentient beings and all of your previous lives in human form around you. This huge assembly of beings joins you in generating the thoughts described in the verses. While chanting the verses, put your palms together at your heart to feel sincerity and respect:

> Great compassionate Protector,
> All-knowing Teacher,
> Field of merit and good qualities vast as an ocean —
> To the Tathagata, I bow.

Paying homage to the Buddha means to show respect to the Buddha's magnificent qualities. It indicates our trust in his ability to teach us the path to awakening and to guide us as we traverse it. The Buddha doesn't need our respect — fully awakened beings don't base their self-esteem on the praise of others! However, we need to develop the ability to recognize, appreciate, and respect the good qualities of others, because doing this opens us to cultivating those same qualities. If we arrogantly think we are learned and holy, we close the door to improving our knowledge and gaining new virtuous qualities.

Why is the Buddha a reliable teacher who is worthy of respect? At the beginning of his *Compendium of Reliable Cognition* (*Pramanasamuccaya*), Dignaga explains that, in previous lives as a bodhisattva, Shakyamuni was intent on benefiting sentient beings. His great compassion spurred him to realize the ultimate nature of reality — the emptiness of inherent existence. Together, his compassion and wisdom enabled him to become a great teacher of sentient beings and a *sugata* ("one gone to bliss," a Buddha). In this way he became the protector of all beings.

The way the Buddha protects us is not by standing guard, building walls, or swooping down like Superman to save us. He protects us by teaching us the Dharma. One meaning of "the Dharma" is protective measures—that is, what to practice and what to avoid in order to create the causes for happiness and to free ourselves from the causes of suffering. The Buddha protects us by teaching us how to protect our own minds from afflictions that motivate actions (karma) that cause rebirth in cyclic existence and miserable experiences. The principal way the Buddha protects us is by teaching us the path, which enables us to learn, contemplate, meditate, and practice the path to attain Buddhahood ourselves.

The Buddha is an omniscient teacher; he knows all that exists. How is this possible? The very nature of the mind is clarity and cognizance; our present inability to know all existence is due to obstructions. Sometimes the obstructions are physical: the wall prevents us from seeing what is on the other side. At other times, the obstruction is due to an impairment in a cognitive faculty—for example, when we are shortsighted, we have difficulties seeing things far away. Sometimes we are limited by the ability of our human cognitive faculties: for example, our human ears cannot hear the sounds that dogs can hear. Other times we have obstacles because our consciousness is clouded by the afflictive and cognitive obscurations that prevent us from knowing things. Because Buddhas have removed both obscurations, all phenomena can easily appear to and be cognized by their minds.

The chief benefit of being all-knowing is that Buddhas know the karma, tendencies, and interests of all living beings. They also know the various paths, their structures, and their practices. This knowledge gives them the ability to guide sentient beings most effectively according to their individual needs at that moment.

The Buddha is the field of merit and good qualities vast as an ocean. Having abandoned everything there is to abandon and realized all that there is to realize, his excellent physical, verbal, and mental qualities are as vast as a huge ocean. Due to his spiritual attainments, Shakyamuni Buddha becomes a field of merit for us, and the virtuous actions that we do in relation to him become extremely potent. The same is true for all other Buddhas.

Reciting verses of homage stimulates us to reflect on the Buddha's good qualities. This uplifts our mind and evokes the aspiration in us to cultivate these same wonderful qualities. Reflecting that we have Buddha nature, we become confident that we can gain the realizations and cessations of a Buddha. Knowing that the Three Jewels can guide us to actualize this aspiration, we take refuge in them and practice their instructions.

Before attaining awakening, Shakyamuni Buddha was an ignorant sentient being like us. By learning, contemplating, and meditating on the Dharma, he attained Buddhahood. We have the same potential; our attainments are contingent on our effort to follow the path. Knowing this broadens our vision of life and encourages us to look beyond the narrow view of human potential that we previously held. We come to know that we have the potential to become fully awakened Buddhas who are of great benefit to sentient beings. We gain confidence that it is possible to eliminate our ignorance, anger, and attachment; it is possible to develop equal love and compassion for all living beings, even those who have harmed us. This is doable if we try. It may not happen quickly, but causes bear their effects; of this we can be sure.

> Through purity, freeing from attachment,
> Through virtue, freeing from the lower realms,
> Unique, supreme ultimate reality —
> To the Dharma that is peace, I bow.

The Dharma Jewel that is our refuge consists of the last two of the four truths for aryas: true cessations and true paths. By realizing true paths — the chief of which is the wisdom directly realizing emptiness — we can gradually eradicate afflictions from our mindstream forever, thereby attaining nirvana, the true cessation of afflictive obscurations and the suffering and unsatisfactory conditions (duhkha) they cause. The Dharma Jewel is the actual refuge that protects us from duhkha. When it has been actualized in our own hearts and minds, we are forever free from cyclic existence and its unsatisfactory circumstances. This is nirvana. Nirvana is not a place we travel to or something that we get from outside and paste onto ourselves.

By also eradicating the cognitive obscurations, we can attain the ultimate true cessation of a fully awakened Buddha. This removal of all defilements such that they can never reappear in our minds is ultimate freedom.

The first two lines of the verse above — "through purity, freeing from attachment, through virtue, freeing from the lower realms" — describe true paths. "Purity" means the absence of inherent existence. Through realizing and continually meditating on the natural purity of our mind — its emptiness of inherent existence — we cut craving, an insidious form of attachment that is the eighth of the twelve links of dependent arising. The Buddha's teaching on the twelve links describes how we repeatedly take rebirth in cyclic existence. The wisdom-realizing emptiness terminates ignorance and the view of a personal identity, which are the root of samsara.

We need many fortunate rebirths in order to develop liberating true paths and liberated true cessations. The cause of such rebirths is virtue: that is, the constructive karma we create motivated by wholesome states of mind such as love, compassion, integrity, consideration for others, faith, generosity, wisdom, and so on. The karma we create—the actions we do—motivated by these virtuous mental states ripens as fortunate rebirths, temporarily freeing us from miserable rebirths in unfortunate realms. Creating virtue also has a freeing effect on our minds right now. We have no guilt, regret, and shame because our thoughts, speech, and deeds have been done without any intention to harm or deceive others. It becomes easier to cultivate concentration because we are not distracted by remorse for our harmful actions. In addition, we feel better about ourselves and our self-esteem increases because we know in our hearts that we are treating others fairly, honestly, and nonviolently.

The last two lines—"unique supreme ultimate reality—to the Dharma that is peace I bow"—explains true cessations. The unique supreme ultimate reality is the emptiness of inherent existence of a mind that has abandoned both the afflictive and the cognitive obscurations. The final true cessation is a type of emptiness, the emptiness of the mind that has eliminated afflictive and cognitive obscurations. From the point of view of their ultimate nature—the emptiness of inherent existence—our minds and the Buddhas' minds are no different. The minds of sentient beings are naturally free from inherent existence, just as the Buddhas' minds are. However, sentient beings' minds are obscured by adventitious defilements, while the Buddhas' minds are totally free from all defilements. In this sense, the emptiness of sentient beings' minds and Buddhas' minds differ. One is the emptiness of a polluted mind; the other is the emptiness of a purified mind.

Liberation and full awakening are true freedom. We usually think freedom means we can do what we want when we want to do it, without interference from the government or other people. While such freedom is certainly desirable, it is a limited type of freedom compared to spiritual freedom. Even when we are fortunate enough to experience this external freedom, our mind remains bound by the three poisons of ignorance, anger, and attachment, along with the host of other afflictions such as jealousy and arrogance that arise from these poisons. These make us miserable now and motivate us to do actions that cause others suffering and create the cause for our own misery in the future. True freedom is internal freedom—liberation, nirvana, the cessation of afflictions. Once attained, that freedom can never be lost or impeded in any way because it does not depend on changeable causes and conditions. This is true happiness, better than all the money and chocolate in the world!

"Peace" is a synonym of "nirvana," which is a state of peace that is the absence of obscurations and the duhkha they create. There are different types of nirvana. Natural nirvana is the emptiness of the mind that all beings have. On the basis of that emptiness, we can attain other types of nirvana.

The nirvana of an arhat—someone who has eliminated the afflictive obscurations and attained liberation—may be a nirvana with or without remainder. Nirvana with remainder is the nirvana of an arhat who still has the remainder of the polluted body he or she took at the time of birth.[2] Nirvana without remainder is an arhat's nirvana after he or she has passed away and left behind that polluted body. The nirvana of a Buddha is nonabiding nirvana, indicating that Buddhas do not abide in cyclic existence because they have eliminated all afflictive obscurations and do not abide in the peaceful state of arhatship because they manifest in the world to benefit sentient beings.

If nirvana seems too abstract to understand easily, think about it this way: Imagine what it would be like to never get angry again. Someone could insult you in public, betray your trust, beat you up, or kill the person you love the most, but your mind would remain peaceful. Of course, with compassion you could decry the person's behavior and try to stop it, but there would be no anger, fear, or hurt in your mind. Wouldn't freedom from anger be wonderful? Then think about what it would feel like to be free of clinging attachment, jealousy, arrogance, self-criticism, and so forth. Not only would we be much happier, but we would affect others in a positive way that would make a difference in their lives.

> Having freed themselves showing the path to freedom, too,
> Well established in the trainings.
> The holy field endowed with good qualities,
> To the Sangha, I bow.

The Sangha Jewel is an arya—a monastic or lay practitioner who has directly realized emptiness on the path of
seeing or above. Aryas may be from any of the three vehicles:
hearer, solitary realizer, or bodhisattva vehicle. Those who
have attained the path of seeing have freed themselves of the
acquired afflictions—afflictions that depend on having stud-
ied incorrect philosophies. Although these aryas no longer
take rebirth under the control of afflictions and karma, they
are not yet completely free from cyclic existence. However,
they will not backslide. Having directly realized the ultimate
nature of phenomena, they can show the path to freedom
to others, teaching them the path accurately from their own
experience.

Aryas are also well established in the three higher trainings of ethical conduct, concentration, and wisdom. These
three become higher trainings when they are done with
refuge in the Three Jewels and with the aspiration to attain
liberation or full awakening. Aryas are well established in
these trainings. They know and understand the scriptures
explaining them and, more importantly, they have trained
their body, speech, and mind in these practices and attained
the correct results. Through both their teachings and their
living example, aryas can show us the path to freedom.

These realized beings are a holy field endowed with good
qualities. By making offerings to them, attending their teachings, asking them questions, and following their example, we
will create great merit and after sufficient practice will gain
realizations ourselves.

A community of four or more fully ordained monastics
represents the Sangha Jewel, and that community is also a
field for our creation of merit because they hold the monastic

precepts established by the Buddhas and perform the rites that the Buddha prescribed for the Sangha community.

Having a full-fledged Sangha community in a place makes that area a "central land," which is one of the eighteen qualities of a precious human life. While lay teachers and lay followers are very important, the monastic community plays a special role in terms of protecting and preserving the teachings from one generation to the next. Holding the precepts helps them to train their minds in the Dharma and to embody the teachings, which inspires others to practice. A simple lifestyle gives monastics more time to study, practice, and teach the Dharma. They have greater flexibility in accepting invitations to teach in other places because they do not need to stay home to care for a family or earn a living to support a family. For example, if I had a family, I would not be able to travel and teach. Even if I gave teachings in a center, the amount of time available to do that and to meet with people privately about their practice would be limited, because my family would require my attention.

In the West, sometimes the word "Sangha" is used for everyone who goes to a Dharma center. This is not the traditional usage of the word, and it can be confusing. For example, when new people are told that we take refuge in the Sangha, they think it refers to taking refuge in the people at the center. But most people at Dharma centers do not have high realizations and some aren't even Buddhists. Although they are our Dharma friends, they cannot guide us on the unmistaken path to liberation. The Sangha that we take refuge in consists of the aryas; they are completely reliable objects of refuge because they have directly realized emptiness and are well trained in ethical conduct, concentration, and wisdom.

Even the monastic community is not the Sangha Jewel, although it represents that Jewel.

Inviting the Three Jewels to Dine

Having paid homage to the Buddha, Dharma, and Sangha in the previous three verses, we now offer the meal. Maintaining the visualization in front of us of Shakyamuni Buddha surrounded by all the Buddhas and bodhisattvas, with Dharma scriptures on jeweled tables beside them, we recite:

> To the supreme teacher, the precious Buddha,
> To the supreme refuge, the holy precious Dharma,
> To the supreme guides, the precious Sangha,
> To all the objects of refuge we make this offering.

With the words "to the supreme teacher, the precious Buddha," we offer the blissful nectar to Shakyamuni Buddha and all other Buddhas. In the scriptures, the Buddha is often referred to as the Teacher because he was the one who first gave teachings in this world—he turned the Dharma wheel by elucidating the path to awakening. His Holiness the Dalai Lama often reminds us that the Buddha is our fundamental or root teacher, and in Chinese Buddhism one of the most often recited chants is "Homage to our fundamental [root] teacher, Shakyamuni Buddha." The main statue or painting in the center of an altar is of the Buddha. Pictures and statues of other deities are placed to the side or slightly lower than the Buddha. This reminds us that all the teachings and the lineages of spiritual mentors originate from the Buddha. For this reason, it is important to respect all Buddhist traditions.

In fact, respecting all other religions is important because all of them teach ethical conduct, love, compassion, and forgiveness. Religious strife in the world is fostered by people who do not understand or adhere to the basic tenets of the religion they purport to be defending.

We have had many teachers in our lives, beginning with our parents, other relatives, or guardians who taught us how to walk and talk, tie our shoes, and be polite to other people. All of these teachers—as well as others who have taught us advanced skills and knowledge—have been incredibly kind and contributed immensely to our well-being. But kind as they are, none of them have the ability to lead us out of the misery of cyclic existence. Of all our teachers, the Buddha is the kindest because he gives us instructions on how to practice the path to awakening. Only Buddhas are incomparable in their wisdom, compassion, power, and skillful means. They have actualized the result of the path and are excellent exemplars in all ways. Our family and friends may love us dearly, they may praise us from here to the heavens, but none of them can teach us how to end our cyclic existence. In fact, many of them inadvertently encourage us to be more involved in cyclic existence and some, in their confusion, encourage us to engage in activities that create destructive karma that will ripen in unfortunate rebirths. For these reasons, the Buddha is the supreme teacher, the most trustworthy of spiritual friends.

Reciting "to the supreme refuge, the holy precious Dharma," we offer the nectar to the Dharma. As mentioned before, the Dharma refuge is the actual refuge that protects us from all unsatisfactory conditions. When true paths are realized and true cessations are actualized in our mindstream, we are forever liberated from afflictions and duhkha. In the *Sutra of the Pristine Wisdom Going Beyond*, the Buddha reminds us: "Since [understanding] the mind is the cause of wisdom, do not look elsewhere for Buddhahood."

Next we offer "to the supreme guides, the precious Sangha." Unlike other religions where the objects of refuge are forever external to us, in Buddhadharma we can become the ultimate refuge objects. By generating true paths and attaining true cessations, we will become aryas, the Sangha Jewel, and our mind will become the Dharma Jewel. After we have thoroughly cleansed our mind of all defilements by meditating on the true paths and completely developed all good qualities, we will become the Buddha Jewel.

Members of the Sangha are good role models for us. Highly revered practitioners as well as those who are not widely known may be part of the arya Sangha. One of my spiritual mentors was especially humble. He wore old robes and scruffy shoes and when his students prepared a high Dharma seat for him, he put a cushion on the floor and taught the Dharma there. People would never recognize him in a crowd, but he was a very high practitioner who had meditated in the mountains for years.

We also benefit by practicing together with the monastic community. By witnessing how they apply Dharma principles to guide their daily activities, we are encouraged and inspired by their example. As Lama Thubten Yeshe used to say, the Sangha gives us a "good visualization." We respect the monastic community not because we like them as individuals or because their robes make them look "holy," but because they hold the precepts set down by the Buddha. When we receive reverence as monastics, we must remember that the respect is directed toward the Buddha, whom we visualize at our hearts, and not to us as individuals.

We learn so much by studying the sutras, commentaries, and treatises, but the Dharma comes alive for us when we witness people implementing it in their daily lives. Slowing down and observing practitioners' behavior is important to increase our learning. We Westerners sometimes tend to be unaware of the opportunity to learn by simply standing back and observing people's behavior, but in Asia this is a vital way that learning occurs.

Needless to say, living near our Dharma teachers, serving them, and assisting them with their virtuous activities are excellent ways to learn by observation. We have the opportunity to observe how they respond to various real-life situations that we may also encounter. Dharma teachers don't always have an easy time: people criticize them, demand attention, and can be very rude to them. Observing how they respond to these situations is witnessing the Dharma in action.

In 1986 when I went to Taiwan to receive *bhiksuni* ordination, I was instructed to keep my eyes lowered and not let my gaze wander across the room to prevent distraction. There was no English translation during our formal training sessions, so to keep up with the others, I had to watch what was happening out of the corner of my eye and follow what everyone else was doing as closely as possible. If their palms were put together in a certain way, I noticed that and did the same. If they began walking with either the left or right foot, I discreetly observed that and copied them. Doing this was a big help to my training. It also enabled me to act in an appropriate way in another culture. Of course, sometimes I was careless, and when the guiding teachers noticed this, they corrected me.

In conclusion, "to all the objects of refuge we make this offering." Now imagine goddesses offering the blissful wisdom nectar to the Three Jewels.[3] They scoop up the nectar from the jeweled vessel and offer it to the entire merit field — the Buddhas, bodhisattvas, and arhats visualized in the space in front of you. Imagine that the holy beings experience great bliss as they accept the blissful wisdom nectar. By chanting these verses and transforming our mind so that it reflects the meaning of the words we're saying, we participate in the beautiful scene imagined around us and include everybody else in it as well.

As an alternative visualization, before offering the blissful wisdom nectar to the merit field, offer it to all the sentient beings imagined around you as far as space exists. Think that the nectar transforms into whatever is needed to fulfill their temporal needs and ultimate aims. Their temporal needs include procuring the four requisites for life — food, clothing, shelter, and medicine. They may need books, a computer, a car, friends, or government officials that work for the benefit of the people. Think that these offerings satisfy the needs of all sentient beings. Then imagine that the nectar transforms into Dharma teachers and texts and whatever else they need to practice the Dharma and fulfill their ultimate goal of liberation or full awakening. Imagine that the minds of all sentient beings are purified and that all beings are endowed with excellent physical, verbal, and mental qualities.

With all sentient beings' needs now being satisfied, together with them we offer the blissful wisdom nectar to the Buddha, Dharma, and Sangha. In addition to offering nectar, imagine all varieties of magnificent offerings filling the sky, and imagine all beings — including ourselves — respectfully offering these to the Three Jewels. Imagining beauty and self-lessly offering it to the holy beings has a profound effect on our mind.

Some people may prefer to offer the nectar to the Buddha, Dharma, and Sangha first, and then to the sentient beings. Personally speaking, I find it helpful to imagine fulfilling the needs of sentient beings first so that they have the mental space and physical well-being to turn their attention to the Three Jewels. I like to think that they too create merit by making offerings to the Three Jewels. This helps my mind when it is irritated with others or upset by the actions of public figures.

If the food has not yet been served, put your palms to-gether at your heart while reciting the verses. If food is already in your bowl or on your plate, put your hands on either side of the dish to offer the food while reciting the offering verses:

> May we and all those around us never be separated from the Triple Gem in any of our lives.
> May we always have the opportunity to make offerings to them.
> And may we continually receive their blessings and inspiration
> To progress along the path.

In this verse, we dedicate the merit from offering the food to the Three Jewels. The first dedication is so that we and everybody around us will never be separated from the Three Jewels in any of our lifetimes. Dedicating in this way is important so that the merit will ripen in our continually meeting the Three Jewels. We want to avoid rebirth in a realm, in a place, or at a time that inhibits us from encountering the Buddha, Dharma, and Sangha. Imagine being born where you have no opportunity to hear about the Three Jewels or receive teachings from qualified spiritual mentors. Or suppose you are reborn at a time when a Buddha has not appeared and turned the wheel of Dharma. Imagine living in a place that lacks religious freedom such that you fear for your life if you are caught reading a Dharma book or moving your lips while reciting mantra.

There are countless hindrances and obstacles to meeting and practicing the Buddha's teachings. To avoid these, we must make strong aspirations and dedications to continually, in all our future rebirths, meet the Three Jewels, to have all conducive conditions to practice the Dharma, and to have the wisdom and joyous effort to take advantage of this fortune. If we think deeply, we will understand that without the Three Jewels we would be completely lost, not only in the present life but in many future lives as well. Reflect on what you would be doing now had you not met the Dharma. Would you create more virtue or nonvirtue? What counterproductive activities might you have gotten involved in? What unwise choices and decisions might you have made? I find thinking about this wakes me up from complacency; it helps me to appreciate my present circumstances and to resolve to use them well, without taking them for granted.

I haven't found a better method than the Buddha's teachings to deal with all the frustrations and temptations that come our way. Without knowing the Dharma, in our confusion we might cope with stress by self-medicating using alcohol, pills, or other intoxicants. Maybe we would deal with dissatisfaction by having an affair. Perhaps we would resort to lying to get what we want.

The Buddha's teachings provide reliable guidance on how to subdue our anger and discontent. They instruct us about how to realize the nature of reality and to cultivate equal love and compassion for all beings. For these reasons, it is important to pray to never be separated from the Three Jewels in any of our lives.

Next we dedicate, "May we always have the opportunity to make offerings to them." In ordinary life, when we appreciate someone, we automatically want to give them gifts and act in ways that make them happy. With this mental state, making offerings to the Three Jewels comes naturally. Furthermore, we appreciate the importance of creating the causes for happiness by engaging in meritorious activities such as making offerings, and we understand that the Buddha, Dharma, and Sangha are an incredible field of merit due to their spiritual attainments. To help us overcome stinginess, we aspire not only to meet the Three Jewels but also to have the mental attitude that takes pleasure in making offerings. Without the opportunity to make offerings to those worthy of respect due to their spiritual realizations, our ability to easily create merit is limited.

The creation of merit is important — it is like fertilizer that enriches our mind so that when the seeds of Dharma teachings are planted in the mind, they will readily grow and produce a crop of realizations. We don't need to be rich to create a lot of merit, because the most important element in making offerings is not the object or the amount we give but our intention. At the time of the Buddha, an elderly, impoverished couple had only one garment between them. Wanting to make an offering to the Buddha, they left it by the roadside where he could pick it up. The material offering was meager, but the merit they created was magnificent due to the power of their sincere, virtuous intention.

Since we eat many times a day, there is a recurring opportunity to cultivate wholesome motivations and create merit by offering our food and drink. The process of visualizing our food dissolving into the emptiness of inherent existence and then reappearing as blissful wisdom nectar is a powerful psychological tool to counteract our ordinary perceptions. Imagining the Buddha at our heart reminds us that we have the potential to become a fully awakened Buddha. For this reason, cultivating the habit of pausing each time before we eat or drink, transforming our mind into virtue by making the offering, not only creates vast merit but also helps us center ourselves spiritually and renew our compassionate motivation frequently during the day.

In this way, may we continuously receive the blessings and inspiration of the Three Jewels to progress along the path. The Tibetan word *jin lab* (*byin rlabs*) can be translated as "blessing" or "inspiration." It actually means "to transform into magnificence." Two conditions are necessary to receive blessings or inspiration: the awakening influence of the Buddhas and our receptivity to receiving it. To hear music on a radio, it is not sufficient for the radio station to broadcast radio waves. Our radio must be turned on. Similarly, the holy beings' awakening influence is always present, but we must be inclined and receptive to receive it. Making offerings and other practices opens our minds and makes them receptive. Requesting inspiration and then sitting back and waiting for a blessing to strike us like lightning doesn't work. We have to make effort and train our mind in the Dharma. When we do, the awakening influence of the Three Jewels can connect with us, aiding us in the gradual process of gaining spiritual realizations.

For example, when we do the Nyung Ne practice—a retreat on Chenrezig, the Buddha of Compassion—each participant receives a little water from the altar vase at the end of each session. We sip the water three times. With the first sip, we imagine that all afflictive emotions are eradicated; with the second, that the cognitive obscurations are overcome; and with the third, that the *dharmakaya*—a Buddha's omniscient mind and its emptiness—is attained. Depending on the sincerity and wisdom with which we contemplate these three, we receive a degree of inspiration or blessing. The way we think blesses our mind; the water we sip is incidental.

> By seeing this food as medicine,
> I will consume it without attachment or complaint,
> Not to increase my arrogance, strength, or good looks,
> But solely to sustain my life.

This verse was written by the great Indian sage of the second and third centuries, Nagarjuna. Similar to the five contemplations, this verse reminds us that the food we are about to eat is like medicine that nourishes our body and keeps it healthy so that we can practice the Dharma. It reminds us to accept the food with gratitude and to eat with contentment, enjoying the food without rushing. Instead of meticulously putting together each mouthful so that it has the right combination of flavors and textures that maximize the pleasure of each bite, we practice contentment, aware of the impermanent nature of the food and of the pleasure we receive from it.

This verse returns us to our motivation for eating. We practice eating without complaining about the food. Complaint arises from aversion and anger; we don't like something and want it to be changed: "This food is too cold. It's too hot. There's not enough protein. You shouldn't serve it in that dish. Why did you make white bread when whole wheat bread is more nutritious? This stale wheat bread tastes like cardboard; I want bread that is soft like cake." We can go on and on, wanting to change this or that about our meal, without ever being satisfied. In the meantime, our complaining and the fuss we create ruins the meal for others. You may have experienced this when dining with friends or relatives in a restaurant and someone makes a scene over the food being undercooked or overcooked.

We love to complain, especially in a monastery where food is one of the few objects of sensual desire we can have. "I don't have a boyfriend, I don't sing or go to the disco, fishing is out, I can't sleep until noon anymore or watch my favorite TV shows. But I still have food!" So a lot of our desire energy goes into what we want to eat.

This verse also reminds us that the purpose of eating is not to increase our arrogance, strength, or good looks. Someone could become arrogant thinking, "Look how wealthy and privileged I am. I eat only the finest gourmet food." Athletes may eat in order to build their muscles, seeking others' admiration: "Look at those muscles. He's so strong." Wanting to impress others with their good looks, some people eat to make their bodies attractive. In ancient times, being plump was a sign of wealth; a man could be proud if his wife were over-weight. Nowadays it's the opposite; people starve themselves to be thin, thinking that being attractive and sexy means they are worthwhile individuals. Meanwhile, they suffer from a diet that is out of balance.

People may also be a little arrogant because they eat organic food. Since organic food is usually more expensive, eating only organic food may be a status symbol. For some it may be a subtle way of saying, "Look, I'm someone who can afford organic food." We may be proud because we are so health conscious and won't allow ourselves to eat that "rubbish, fast food." Our self-centered attitude can twist anything to become a reason for arrogance.

Other people may be proud because they are vegan, and some people are what could be called "born-again vegetarians" due to the enthusiasm with which they push everyone to stop eating meat. While I believe vegetarianism protects life and prevents ill effects in the environment, harping about it to others does not create harmony. People must come to the conclusion to be vegetarian or vegan themselves.

Overall, these verses remind us to eat with the proper motivation: to accept food without attachment, to eat without complaint or arrogance. We eat to keep our body alive. Having received the food through the kindness of countless sentient beings, we have the responsibility to repay the kindness of others by paying it forward in whatever ways we can. Each of us has unique skills and talents; we must use them to benefit others and make a positive contribution to others' lives. For monastics, this entails keeping our precepts, studying and practicing the Dharma well, and serving sentient beings through teaching, counseling, and engaging in social service projects. Ultimately we repay others' kindness by progressing on the path and becoming fully awakened Buddhas.

Since we chant these verses every day, it is easy to let our mind wander and forget the meaning of what we say. But if we try to lock our attention onto each word we chant and think of its meaning, these contemplations and verses have a powerful effect on our mind.

Offerings on the Go: A Simplified Version of Offering Food and Drink

Sometimes you may be in a situation where you cannot recite the contemplations out loud or do not have time to slowly recite the verses—for example, you are dining at a restaurant or sharing food with friends or family who are not Buddhist. In this case, while your companions chat, mentally recite an abbreviated version of the offering verses. Think, "I will offer this food to Shakyamuni Buddha, who is the embodiment of all the Buddhas, Dharma, and Sangha, in order to attain full awakening for the sake of all sentient beings." Say OM AH HUM to consecrate the food, and think of it as becoming very pure, like sweet nectar that tastes delicious and gives bliss similar to what the Buddha experiences. This nectar is completely beyond the usual ordinary appearance of food. Offer the food with the three following verses, and imagine that the Buddha at your heart experiences bliss as you eat:

To the supreme teacher, the precious Buddha,
To the supreme refuge, the holy precious Dharma,
To the supreme guides, the precious Sangha,
To all the objects of refuge we make this offering.

May we and all those around us never be separated from
the Triple Gem in any of our lives.
May we always have the opportunity to make offerings
to them.
And may we continually receive their blessings and
inspiration
To progress along the path.

By seeing this food as medicine,
I will consume it without attachment or complaint,
Not to increase my arrogance, strength, or good looks,
But solely to sustain my life.

At the Abbey, we recite this shorter version before breakfast and medicine meal (our name for dinner, which some
people eat and others do not). At lunch, which is our main
meal, we recite the five contemplations and chant all the
verses. You may choose which verses to recite depending on
which meal is your main meal and with whom you are eating.

4

Dinner Table Dharma
Family Meals

Eating together regularly as a family — be it at breakfast, lunch, or dinner — has many benefits for children, teenagers, parents, and grandparents. Conversations during mealtimes give family members the opportunity to connect, bond, and learn from one another. To do that, everyone must turn off their electronic devices for a while and pay attention to the people sitting in front of them. This can be challenging nowadays, but it is important to give ourselves the chance to connect in real time with living people who have feelings.

Building Skills for the Future

Sharing meals engenders feelings of belonging, warmth, security, love, and caring. It also provides time for each person to talk about his or her day and share any news or discuss current events. Simply asking, "What did you learn today?" or "What interesting activities did you do today?" at a meal opens the door for parents and children to talk, and enables children to connect with parents on a deeper level about things that are important to them. Asking your children, "Did you face any challenges today?" opens the door for them to open up and share their feelings as well as seek guidance on how to handle the situations they encounter.

It's good to begin having open discussions where parents listen to their children when the children are young. That builds trust so that when the children become teenagers, they know they can communicate openly with their parents without being judged or told what to do.

Sometimes parents may seed the discussion by sharing an event from their day or something they heard or read about. They then ask the kids, "What do you think is a good way to look at this?" or "What ideas do you have for how to handle this situation?" This builds confidence as children are able to express their ideas, and parents skillfully model the art of listening. Sharing family meals can help lessen normal day-to-day frictions and create meaningful family traditions.

Studies show that children and teenagers' academic performance improves when their family eats together. Dinnertime conversations boost vocabulary even more than reading aloud to children. Research shows that preteens and teenagers who eat five or more meals a week with a parent are more likely to understand, acknowledge, and follow the boundaries and guidance of their parents. They are also less likely to be involved in risky behaviors that cause parents concern, such as binge drinking and illegal drug use, violence, eating disorders, and having problems in school. Frequent meals together have a positive impact on youngsters' values, motivations, identity, and self-awareness.

Even when each family member's schedule, activities, and commitments are complicated, it's important to make sharing meals together a top family priority. Parents have to take the lead on this and arrange their schedules accordingly. Simply saying "Life is too hectic" and abandoning quality time with your children is setting yourself up for difficulties when the young ones become teenagers and young adults.

In addition, family meals tend to be more nutritious and less expensive than eating on the run. They improve children's eating habits and provide the perfect opportunity for parents to model appropriate manners. Nowadays children often miss out on learning how to plan and prepare meals. Parents can teach them to be self-reliant by getting them involved in kitchen skills appropriate to their age, such as simple menu planning, helping with the grocery shopping, setting the table, making salad, chopping veggies, cooking, and baking desserts. Cleaning up after the meal can also be a group activity. All of these prepare children to take care of themselves when they leave home. Learning to help around the house will also save them from difficulties when they later have roommates and partners of their own. If your children learn to be team players and help with family chores, they will get along much better with others when they establish households for themselves.

Instilling Ethics Early

Offering meals together is a wonderful family tradition. During my travels, I stayed with a family with small children. Dinner was their family meal. The children helped set the table, and after the food was placed on the table, everyone held hands. The children had memorized the offering prayer and they led the recitation. I've found more than once that the children learn the offering verses more quickly than their parents! The kids are eager to recite them and show what they have learned. The children then ask about the Buddha, Dharma, and Sangha, and their questions about the Three Jewels and why we offer our meals to them is a good way to introduce children to the Buddha's teachings.

Another way to use food to introduce children to the Three Jewels is to have the children help you offer food on the altar in your home. When I stayed with a friend of mine, I witnessed a lovely family custom. The mother and her young daughter bowed to the Buddha each morning in front of the altar in their home. Then Mom gave the child some cookies or fruit to offer to the Buddha, which the daughter very carefully did. After she "gave the Buddha a present," the Buddha "gave her a present" in return—a small treat or something the child liked. Then they would chant OM MANI PADME HUM—the mantra of Chenrezig, the Buddha of Compassion—together. Needless to say, the daughter loved giving the Buddha presents and grew up to be a serious Buddhist practitioner herself.

Some parents who are Buddhist hesitate to introduce their children to the Dharma, often because when they were children religion was forced on them. Not wanting to pressure their own children, they don't speak about Buddhism or teach it to their children, saying that they want to let their children decide what religion to follow—if any—when they are older.

Although I agree that religion should never be forced on anyone, not introducing children to the Dharma when they are young is a disadvantage for the children. Children need ethical guidelines. Discussing these, especially in relation to how they interact with their siblings, classmates, and adults, is a great opportunity to talk about the ten nonvirtues and the ten virtues as well as karma and its effects. These teachings are practical—they are not dogmatic and can be taught to children so that they see the immediate benefits of treating others with respect and acting generously. Children are also curious about life, and it's important to answer their questions with sincerity and expose them to new ideas. They want to know what happens to their dog, cat, or hamster when it dies. They look to their parents and other adults to understand how to respond to the death of a loved one and what to do to help the deceased.

Buddhist methods for working with anger and cultivating love and compassion can easily be taught to children, beginning at a very early age. Just helping kids learn to identify their emotions and label them gives them the ability to communicate their feelings and needs. It enables them to see that other people also have feelings, and with that awareness parents can teach their children how to empathize and care about others.

Children also benefit from knowing that their parents meditate. So often parents tell their kids to sit down and be quiet, but the children never see their parents model that behavior! But when they know that meditation time is quiet time and they see Mom and Dad sitting peacefully, it's a powerful role model for the children. Young children also like to be with their parents during these relaxed, peaceful times. My young niece liked to come in the room and color during my morning meditation time, and sometimes I would rub her back while reciting mantras. This was a quiet way of bonding.

5

Mindful Eating

L IKE ALL ACTIVITIES in our life, eating gives us the
possibility to be vividly alive and present, free from the
three poisons of confusion, attachment, and anger. There
is an opportunity to transform this neutral action into one
that creates merit and brings Dharma happiness in the
present. Most cultures treasure eating not only for its sensual pleasure but also because people bond by sharing food
together. By nourishing each other with food and human
connection, life continues. But to what extent do we take
this opportunity and pay attention to both the food and the
people we share it with?

Being Out to Lunch

Have you ever noticed how much people like to talk about
food? In my family, it was a favorite topic of conversation:
who cooked what, how good it tasted, what ingredients were
used, and how it was prepared. When my family went out
to eat at a restaurant with their friends, they would spend
at least half an hour deciding what to order. They would ask
the waiter or waitress what he or she recommended, and if

it were possible to substitute one ingredient for another so it would be exactly what they liked.

Even when ordering takeout, my family took a long time to decide which restaurant to choose. Do you feel like eating Chinese, Indian, Thai, or Mexican? Or maybe keep it simple and get a pizza or fast food? Was the food good the last time we got takeout from that restaurant? (We never ordered takeout from French or Italian restaurants; we dressed up and went there on special occasions.) Once the type of food was decided, another long discussion ensued on which dishes we would order. What was their specialty? Would we share dishes or would each person order his or her own dish? Who wanted spicy and who didn't?

Everyone enjoyed these discussions (except me; I was hungry and just wanted to eat). But I noticed that as soon as the food was served — whether we were at home or at a restaurant — nobody really tasted it (unless it was bad, in which case a polite fuss ensued and the food was sent back). We talked while we ate, and while we commented on the taste of the food, nobody really slowed down and tasted it. We ate quickly and the food was gone. Then we went on to discuss for twenty minutes what to eat for dessert. Needless to say, dinners at home weren't so extended. Mom was a good cook, but, as they say, there were two options for dinner at home: take it or leave it. But at home, too, we seldom really tasted the food.

Eating with a Virtuous Mind

Having prepared the mind, transformed the food into blissful wisdom nectar, and offered the food, how do we eat it?

As mentioned above, one visualization is to imagine a small Buddha made of light at our heart and offer each spoonful of nectar to him. The Buddha radiates light that fills our entire body, bringing a deep sense of satisfaction. Feeling satisfied and content while eating overcomes craving and dissatisfaction, emotions that we often wrestle with when eating mindlessly.

At the Abbey we eat breakfast and lunch in silence. A bell is rung toward the end of the meal, and after that, we talk for a while before chanting the dedication. The silence enables us to focus on the visualization or continue with the five contemplations. Speaking gives us the opportunity to connect as a community.

Many people talk about being mindful while eating. What is mindfulness? What many people call mindfulness is actually bare attention—paying attention to and closely observing our experience. This is another tool to help us overcome craving and dissatisfaction while eating, and it can be practiced whether we eat slowly or quickly.

The Sanskrit and Pali words for "mindfulness" can also be translated as "remembering." With mindfulness we hold in our minds the values, principles, and precepts that guide our actions and speech. With introspective awareness, another mental factor that is often paired with mindfulness, we observe our body, speech, and mind to see if they are adhering to our values, principles, and precepts or if our minds have gotten distracted by restlessness, drowsiness, or some other distraction.

In the case of eating, the five contemplations are five mindfulness practices to do while we eat. We practice being mindful of the causes and conditions and the kindness of others by which we have received the food. We take care to ensure that our mind remains virtuous while we eat, without letting it stray into attachment, complaining, or confusion. We remember to regard the food as wondrous medicine that nourishes our body. We are mindful that having nourished our body, we want to use it as the vehicle to accomplish our ultimate goal—Buddhahood. To do this, we strengthen our motivation to generate bodhicitta and the wisdom realizing emptiness.

For many years I led retreats at a Buddhist retreat center that hosted activities for practitioners from the Theravada, Zen, and Tibetan traditions. Friends who worked there told me that they could tell which Buddhist tradition people followed by the way they ate. The Vipassana[1] and Theravada practitioners enter the dining room walking very slowly. They closely observe each step and slowly and mindfully serve food from the buffet and sit down. They pick up the fork or spoon slowly, mindfully put food in their mouths, and chew it slowly and thoroughly. The meal lasts forty-five minutes to over an hour because they pay attention to and experience the taste and texture of every bite.

Zen practitioners walk in, sit down, and chant their prayers quickly. They eat quickly, and the meal is over in ten minutes. They chant the dedication and leave. They focus on eating because everyone must finish their meal soon. There is no time to be picky or to crave different foods.

Practitioners of Tibetan Buddhism enter the room, chant their verses, serve the food, and eat at a normal pace. All three groups eat in silence and clean up in silence.

Through this example we see that while each tradition practices in a different way, the purpose is the same. All of these ways help practitioners to subdue their attachment to food. By serving the food and eating slowly, Theravada and Vipassana practitioners maintain awareness of the taste and texture of the food and the sensation of the food in their mouths. When the mind is focused solely on this awareness, attachment does not arise. Zen practitioners eat very quickly, so there is no time to be attached to food and ponder whether they like it or not. Everybody has to finish at the same time, so they must keep up the pace. Tibetan practitioners who eat at a normal speed also do so with introspective awareness, in this case focusing on offering each spoonful to the Buddha, who radiates purifying light that fills their bodies and minds.

Personally speaking, I believe our motivation for eating is the key factor in transforming the action of eating into Dharma practice. When we recognize that we are able to eat due to the kindness of the sentient beings involved in the many activities necessary for a plate of food to arrive in front of us, attachment to food is easily replaced by gratitude toward sentient beings. When we contemplate that we have food now because in previous times we practiced generosity, we are inspired to eat with a virtuous mind to create constructive karma that will continue our good circumstances. We also realize that by accepting and eating this food, we have the responsibility to pay it forward by benefiting others with our study, meditation, and service work.

Eating is a good time to notice the difference between our expectation, which is a conceptual consciousness, and the actual experience, which is a nonconceptual consciousness. When we look at the dishes on a buffet or our plate, a conceptual image of what each dish will taste like appears in our mind. Due to attachment, our mental consciousness forms a conceptual image of how delicious the chocolate cake will taste—rich, creamy, sweet, soft. But when we put it in our mouth, the actual taste and texture don't always match our expectation. The taste is a bit off—there is coffee or maybe coconut mixed in and we don't like that taste. The cake is not as sweet as we had hoped it would be, and it's also a bit dry. Occasionally things taste better than our expectation, but not always. We are often disappointed. However, when we place our mindfulness on the five contemplations, this dissatisfied attitude is replaced by acceptance and gratitude.

When eating I sometimes focus on the impermanence of the food to counteract attachment. Once I've put food into my mouth and started chewing, it no longer looks appealing. Unless someone is starving, no one would want to eat a strawberry that I've chewed and spit out. Then the strawberry gets digested and comes out the other end as poop. I then generalize this to all samsaric pleasures, which are impermanent and don't last. Thinking like this isn't depressing, it's realistic. Instead of building up unrealistic expectations that cannot be fulfilled—which definitely makes us unhappy—we develop an awareness of the disadvantages of samsara. This strengthens our determination to be liberated from samsara, which spurs us to understand the nature of reality. Exploring the nature of reality is very interesting and intriguing; our life is never boring when we do this.

When we chew food slowly, sometimes we enjoy the taste more, but sometimes we get tired of chewing the same thing and our mind longs for a new burst of flavor with a new bite. Attachment to sensual pleasure leaves us dissatisfied and seeking "more and better." From a Buddhist viewpoint, this unsatisfactory situation is due not to defects in the sense objects but to our craving, which exaggerates their good qualities and mistakenly believes that the pleasure from sensory objects will bring us lasting happiness. Dharma practice is directed toward eliminating craving and attachment and deriving happiness from internal mental states such as compassion and wisdom. These internal states are based on a realistic perspective and are beneficial for ourselves and others.

6

Eating without Harm

NUMEROUS BOOKS have been written on what to eat and how to have a balanced diet. Of the many ways to do this, each person, family, or group of people will choose a way that suits them when they are ready to do this.

It seems that more people worldwide are becoming vegetarian for a variety of reasons. As Buddhists, we avoid eating meat to reduce the killing of animals, which brings direct suffering to the animals and plants the seeds of the nonvirtuous action of killing on the mindstreams of those who killed them. Raising cattle harms the environment by leading to soil pollution and the generation of methane gas from their manure. In addition, cattle consume disproportionate quantities of grain to produce comparatively little meat. Meat animals are also fed many hormones, antibiotics, and other chemicals, and fish absorb harmful chemicals from polluted rivers, lakes, and streams. Human beings imbibe all these pollutants by consuming the animals' flesh.

It has been said that by eating meat, some of the animal's energy of ignorance, fear, anxiety, or anger that is stored in their body is transmitted to the human being who eats the flesh. We now know that different hormones and other substances are produced when various emotions are felt. Consuming these hormones when eating meat could adversely affect people.

His Holiness the Dalia Lama often says that if you can manage, being vegetarian is best. If you can't be fully vegetarian, then try to eat less meat. His Holiness calls himself a "part-time vegetarian" and explains that some years ago he was fully vegetarian, but at one point became ill. At that time, his doctor advised him to eat a little meat for health reasons. Before eating meat, His Holiness recites mantras to benefit the animal who gave up its life, and he dedicates merit so that the animal will take a good rebirth, meet with the Dharma, and actualize the path in future lives. Likewise, it's beneficial if people who eat meat pray to repay the kindness of those whose bodies they eat. After all, we wouldn't give up our lives for someone else's lunch, so it's imperative to appreciate their sacrifice and dedicate merit to benefit these beings in future lives in whatever forms we and they may appear. In particular, we should practice well so we will be capable of teaching them the Dharma and leading them on the path to awakening in future lives.

His Holiness also recommends that those who eat meat consume the meat from larger animals rather than smaller ones. In that way the loss of one life will lead to many meals, whereas if you consume smaller animals, such as fish, clams, shrimp, or scallops, many living beings die for one human meal.

Some people worry that being vegetarian is not good for their health. I have been vegetarian for about forty-five years, since I was twenty-two or twenty-three, and it hasn't harmed my health. It is easy to learn to eat wisely and stay healthy on a vegetarian diet. Other sources of protein are plentiful and you can also take vitamins.

The monastic community at the Abbey is vegetarian, whether we eat at the Abbey or visit family and friends who eat meat. All our guests are vegetarian while they are with us. Although we advocate vegetarian diets, we are not "born-again vegetarians" and do not insist that others permanently change their eating habits to correspond to our beliefs.

Some years ago a visitor to the Abbey asked why we didn't consume organic produce, milk from cows that graze in open fields, and eggs from free-range chickens. He believed that if we didn't do that, then we should be vegan and not consume any animal products at all. He was quite emphatic about this.

We do grow a small portion of organic produce in our garden, and we only use eggs that are not fertilized to avoid killing. But organic produce, free-range eggs, and milk from open-range cows are more expensive. If someone can afford such choices, it's better to eat these. But we monastics are renunciates. We don't buy food; we eat only the food that is offered to us. People are already giving to us with generous hearts; it would be disrespectful to ask that they offer expensive food that they do not even buy for themselves. From time to time, people do bring organic produce — especially in the fall when they share vegetables from their own gardens and fruit from the fruit trees around their homes.

Many Abbey residents are practitioners of *kriya*, or action tantra, which includes deity practices such as Thousand-Armed Chenrezig, White Tara, Green Tara, Medicine Buddha, and Manjushri. One kriya tantra precept is to avoid "black foods": meat (including chicken and fish), fertilized eggs, garlic, onions, scallions, leeks, and radishes. Eastern and Western cultures view foods such as garlic differently. In many Asian cultures, onion and garlic are said to increase the energy of desire and to disrupt the flow of the subtle winds, or *qi*, in the body. In the West, garlic is said to be medicinal. We follow the view that corresponds with the Eastern tradition.

When some people hear that we don't use onion and garlic, they exclaim, "Your food must have no taste! How can you possibly cook good food without onions?" But when they come to the Abbey and eat with us, they are surprised to learn that it is possible to make very tasty food without onions and garlic. Once, when I was leading a retreat in Mexico, I reminded the organizers to prepare vegetarian meals without onions and garlic. They gasped in horror, "Over a hundred people are coming to the retreat. They'll complain if they have to eat tasteless food!" I said, "Well, let's try." We did, and no one complained. In fact, they were quite happy.

I'm not advocating this way of eating for everybody; this is simply what we do at the Abbey. Eating onions, garlic, and scallions does not involve killing so people can consume them without harming others. In short, people's diet will depend not only on their spiritual practice but also on their culture, health requirements, and the food that is available at reasonable prices in the place where they live. The most important principle to remember is to avoid harming others as much as possible.

7

After-Dinner Mints
Dedications and Reflections

A FTER FINISHING lunch, monastics and guests at the Abbey chant verses that encapsulate the practices of making offerings, purification, and dedication:

OM UCCHISHTA PANDI ASHIBHYA SVAHA
TAYATA GATE GATE PARAGATE PARASAMGATE
    BODHI SVAHA

CHOMDENDAY DESHIN SHEGPA DRACHOMPA YANG-
DAGPAR TSOGPAY SANGYE RINCHEN OKYI GYALPO
MAY O RABTU SELWA LA CHAG TSAL LO
(repeat three times)

NAMA SAMANTA PRABHA RAJAYA TATHAGATAYA
ARHATE SAMYAKSAM BUDDHAYA NAMO MANJUSHRIYE
KUMARA BHUTAYA BODHISATTVAYA MAHASATTVAYA
MAHA KARUNIKAYA TAYATA OM NIRALAMBHA
NIRABHASE JAYA JAYE LAMBHE MAHAMATE DAKSHI
DAKSHENAM MEPARISHVADHA SVAHA
(repeat three times)

May all those who offered me food attain happiness of total peace. May all those who offered me drink, who served me, who received me, who honored me, or who made offerings to me attain happiness which is total peace.

May all those who scold me, make me unhappy, hit me, attack me with weapons, or do things up to the point of killing me attain the happiness of awakening. May they fully awaken to the unsurpassed, perfectly accomplished state of Buddhahood.

By the merit of offering food, may they have a good complexion, magnificence, and strength. May they find foods having hundreds of tastes and live with the food of samadhi.

By the merit of offering drink, may their afflictions, hunger, and thirst be pacified. May they possess good qualities such as generosity and take a rebirth without any sickness or thirst.

The one who gives, the one who receives, and the generous action are not to be observed as truly existent. By giving with impartiality, may the benefactors attain perfection.

By the power of being generous, may they become Buddhas for the benefit of sentient beings, and through generosity, may all the beings who have not been liberated by previous conquerors be liberated.

By the merit of this generosity, may the *naga* kings, gods having faith in the Dharma, leaders who support religious freedom, benefactors, and others living in the area live long, enjoy good health and prosperity, and attain lasting happiness.

Due to this virtue, may all beings complete the collections of merit and wisdom. May they attain the two Buddha bodies resulting from merit and wisdom.

Feeding the Hungry Ghosts

Based on an event during the Buddha's time, the custom began to make a food offering to the hungry ghosts (*preta*) after finishing our meal. A mother hungry ghost was stealing human babies to feed her children. When the Buddha asked her why she was doing this and causing so much suffering to others, the mother preta explained, "I have five hundred hungry children who are crying for food, and they depend on me to feed them." To protect the human babies and to fulfill the needs of the mother preta and her children, the Buddha promised that if she abandoned killing and became vegetarian, his disciples would feed her and her children every day so that she wouldn't have to kill other living beings.

In Chinese monasteries, the preta offering is made before the meal, when seven grains of rice are blessed and taken outside. In Tibetan and Himalayan monasteries, the preta offering is made at the conclusion of the meal because hungry ghosts cannot partake of fresh food; their karma obscures them from seeing fresh food as edible.

To make this offering, with your left hand take a small portion of food from your plate—usually bread, rice, or another grain—something that will stick together and can easily be shaped. Squeeze it in your left hand by making a fist, so that the rice ball becomes as long as your fist and has the imprints of your fingers in its side. If your meal didn't contain food that can be shaped in this way, then take a little bread, briefly lick it so the pretas can perceive it as edible, and then squeeze it into the proper shape. Lift your left hand and say the mantra,

OM UCCHISHTA PANDI ASHIBHYA SVAHA

and the Perfection of Wisdom mantra,

TAYATA GATE GATE PARAGATE PARASAMGATE
BODHI SVAHA

Imagine the offering dissolves into emptiness and is transformed into limitless blissful wisdom nectar with the ability to completely satisfy the hunger and thirst of the pretas. With your right hand, snap your fingers to call the pretas, and then toss the offering onto a plate in the middle of the table. (When the meal is taken in the prayer hall of Tibetan monasteries, the monastics toss the offering on the floor.) Imagine the pretas consume the offering. Their hunger is relieved, and they feel satisfied. When cleaning up after the meal, put the preta offerings outside. Because the pretas develop the habit of coming every day, monastic communities make the offering daily.

Purifying Misdeeds

Now we purify any negativity we may have accumulated by not practicing well, yet consuming food offered by those with faith in the Dharma. This is especially important for monastics to do. While reciting the following praise and mantra, imagine light radiating from the Buddha visualized in front of you or on top of your head. The brilliant yet gentle light streams into you, purifying any misdeeds on your part.

CHOMDENDAY DESHIN SHEGPA DRACHOMPA YANG-
DAGPAR TSOGPAY SANGYE RINCHEN OKYI GYALPO
MAY O RABTU SELWA LA CHAG TSAL LO
(repeat three times)

This Tibetan verse means "I bow to the *bhagavan*, the Tathagata, the arhat, the fully awakened Buddha, Victor of Precious Light, Very Clear Fire Light." In Sanskrit, this Buddha's name is Ratnaprabharaja Jvalanakaraprakatita. Then chant the Sanskrit mantra:

NAMA SAMANTA PRABHA RAJAYA TATHAGATAYA
ARHATE SAMYAKSAM BUDDHAYA NAMO MANJUSHRIYE
KUMARA BHUTAYA BODHISATTVAYA MAHASATTVAYA
MAHA KARUNIKAYA TADYATA OM NIRALAMBHA
NIRABHASE JAYA JAYE LAMBHE MAHAMATE DAKSHI
DAKSHENAM MEPARISHVADHA SVAHA
(repeat three times)

A translation of this mantra is as follows: "Homage to the all-powerful king, the Tathagata, arhat, the fully awakened Buddha. Homage to the princely Manjushri, the bodhisattva, the great being, the great compassionate one; thus, OM, free of supports [or objects], free of false appearances, victorious, victorious, possessed of great mind, wisest of the wise, be kind to me. May it be so."

Dedicating for Friends and Foes

The next set of verses contains dedication prayers from Tibetan Buddhism. Here we dedicate for all sentient beings in general, and specifically for the people who have offered food to us. At Sravasti Abbey, this includes all our guests as well as those who live in other places who have offered money to the Friends of Sravasti Abbey groups in Coeur d'Alene and Spokane that buy and transport groceries on their behalf. It also includes people who purchase food online that is sent to us and those who bake homemade goods that they package and mail to us. We appreciate the kindness of all of these people and dedicate for their well-being and spiritual progress. This reaffirms the close relationship between those who sincerely practice the Dharma and the benefactors who sustain their lives so that they can practice.

In a family setting, dedicate for the family members whose salaries were used to purchase food and for the family members who shopped and prepared the food. Children who set the table or help with cleanup will be happy knowing that the family is dedicating for them as well.

> May all those who offered me food attain happiness of total peace. May all those who offered me drink, who served me, who received me, who honored me, or who made offerings to me attain happiness which is total peace.

Nirvana is the happiness of total peace. Those who offered me food include the people who grew, harvested, transported, or packaged it as well as those who bought it, prepared the meal, arranged the food on the buffet, and cleaned up afterward. All those people — many of whom are strangers — have benefited us.

"Those who received me" refers to people who have invited us for a meal. For monastics, it means people who offer Sangha-dana — a meal to the Sangha — in their homes or at a restaurant. "Those who honored me" are people who respect the Sangha. The respect they show is directed toward the precepts existing in the mindstreams of monastics, not to members of the Sangha as individuals. There is no reason for monastics to become proud when people offer respect. When others respect us it benefits them, not us, for they accumulate merit. Our job is to remain humble.

"Those who have made offerings to me" includes anyone who has offered us any of the requisites for life — food, clothing, shelter, and medicine. We also dedicate for those who have made other offerings — for example, offering the video camera that allows us to record and stream teachings, the computers that enable us to write books and assemble prayer books, the forest equipment that lets us care for our forest and meadows, and vehicles that enable us to go to Spokane and other venues to teach and to run errands in our local town of Newport. The list goes on; everything we see and touch at the Abbey came due to the kindness of others.

Lay practitioners dedicate for the well-being of their employers who pay their salary. We usually think that since we earned the money, there would be no reason to thank our employers. But probing more deeply, we see that we benefit from having a job. Instead of thinking, "I worked for this, I earned it. It's mine," think, "At birth I came into this world without anything, and look at everything I have now! I have it because of the kindness of others who gave it to me." It's amazing, isn't it? We owned nothing when we were born, yet think about everything we have used and consumed since then. All of these things came due to the kindness and efforts of others.

May they "attain happiness which is total peace" could refer to the nirvana of an arhat, but it's better if we dedicate for them to attain the nonabiding nirvana of a fully awakened Buddha.

> May all those who scold me, make me unhappy, hit me, attack me with weapons, or do things up to the point of killing me attain the happiness of awakening. May they fully awaken to the unsurpassed, perfectly awakened state of Buddhahood.

In the first verse, we dedicated for the awakening of everyone who has been kind to us. This verse asks us to do something more difficult: to dedicate for those who have harmed us, people we would normally consider enemies and threats to our well-being. Usually we want people who interfere with our happiness or inflict suffering on us to suffer in return. Spitefully we "dedicate" for them to have a taste of their own medicine, as if their suffering would make us feel better. Of course, it never does. That way of thinking sinks us into a ditch of frustrated mental pain. Needless to say it is not appropriate for someone who is receiving offerings due to the kindness of others.

Seeing this, we realize that we must change our attitude and release the critical, judgmental attitude that thinks, "People who harm me or treat me poorly are disgusting. They are evil and irredeemable, and I have the right to hate them forever." For our own benefit as well as the benefit of others, we must soften this attitude and become more tolerant and less self-centered. Why? Because when we are angry and hold a grudge, we're the ones who suffer the most. The other person continues to live their life while we remain stuck in angry ruminations about the suffering and injustice of what they said or did to us.

Releasing our anger doesn't mean that what the other person did or said was okay; it may not have been. We can say that their actions or words were inappropriate or harmful, but for our own well-being we must forgive them. Forgiving simply means letting go of our anger. We may choose not to forgive, but in doing so our anger and arrogance are condemning us to a life of inner malaise and turmoil.

What effect does holding a grudge have on our Dharma practice? Have you ever heard of a Buddha who seeks revenge and rejoices in the misery others? In the *Jataka Tales*, which contains stories of the Buddha's previous lives as a bodhisattva, we never read, "When the Buddha was a bodhisattva he decided to take revenge on somebody who harmed him." To the contrary, all the stories are about him finding a way to communicate with the person who harmed him and to benefit that person in one way or another. Clearly retaliation is not a step on the path to awakening!

People who scold us, who shout at us or point out our faults, who make up lies about us or criticize us to our face — these are the same people who, in another lifetime, have been kind to us, who served us, honored us, and made offerings to us. Similarly, those who are kind to us in this lifetime have harmed us in previous lives. Seeing these ever-changing relationships, it is impossible to say someone is a true enemy.

We also dedicate for people who have habits or attitudes that we find irritating or even intolerable. Perhaps they whine and complain a lot, "The world is so unfair! I'm unhappy and it's other people's fault." Our dedication also includes people who hit us, as well as those who terrorize or assault us. We usually put labels on these people—"They are evil monsters"—and believe that this label indicates the sum value of their lives. Change the situation and look at it the reverse way: Would we like others to judge us based entirely on the worst thing we ever did? Of course not! We are much more than our misdeeds; we have the Buddha nature and incredible potential. So do those people. I have learned this from over two decades of working with incarcerated people.

In regard to "those who hit me, attack me with weapons, or do things up to the point of killing me"—even if those people are trying to victimize us, we can refuse to be a victim. It is our mind—not someone else's actions—that makes us a victim. We have the choice to refuse to be a victim by not adopting a victim mentality. Being a victim indicates our mind is frozen in the past. We have generated certain conceptions about what happened, who we were, who the other person was, and then clung to those thoughts as if they were objectively true. In fact, what happened in the past is not as important as how we think about it now. While we can't change what happened, we can change how we view and interpret those events now. This is the beauty of the Buddha's teachings: they show us how to dissolve our false conceptions and to see people and events in a realistic and beneficial way.

Happy people don't harm other people; unhappy people who are confused about how to create the causes of happiness do. Instead of focusing on what they did to us, we can think about the unhappiness they felt that made them act in that way. They were suffering and had unmet physical or emotional needs. Shouldn't they be objects of our compassion, not of our anger? It makes sense to dedicate for the well-being of the people who harm us, because if they were happy and content, they wouldn't be doing those actions that we find objectionable.

Furthermore, their actions interfere only with our happiness of this life. The worst they can do to us is kill us, which, of course, is terrible, but they cannot make us take a lower rebirth, which is even worse. As Shantideva, the eighth-century Indian sage who wrote *Engaging in the Bodhisattvas' Deeds*, reminds us, our own disturbing emotions and destructive actions are the causes of unfortunate rebirths. They are the real enemies who harm us, not other people. Therefore we must work hard to abolish our self-centered attitude, as well as our self-grasping ignorance and the afflictions that arise from it. Since it will take us a while to free ourselves forever from these, in the meantime we can engage in the practice of fortitude that Shantideva explains so beautifully in chapter 6 of his book. His Holiness the Dalai Lama's book *Healing Anger* and my book *Working with Anger* are based on Shantideva's wise and compassionate words.

Dedicating for all those who have interfered with our happiness or caused us harm to attain the happiness of awakening helps us to release our victim mentality, anger, and self-pity. We practice wishing them well: May they purify all their destructive actions and have conducive circumstances to meet and practice the Dharma. May they fully awaken to the unsurpassed, perfectly awakened state of Buddhahood. May their minds be completely purified of every last defilement and may they gain all Dharma realizations from the beginning to the end of the path. May they actualize their potential to become Buddhas, attaining all the inconceivable excellent qualities of the fully awakened beings.

This is a process of training ourselves so that in our mind and heart—not simply by our mouth—we wish them well. This applies to all those we fear and hate—be they political figures we have never met or the kid who hit us on the playground when we were in first grade.

Pacifying Hunger and Thirst: Dedicating the Merit of Offering Food and Drink

By the merit of offering food, may they have a good complexion, magnificence, and strength. May they find foods having hundreds of tastes and live with the food of samadhi.

Now we dedicate the merit our supporters accumulated from offering food and drink. First we wish that they always have a good complexion—that they are physically attractive. The cause for having an attractive body in future lives is practicing fortitude in this life. When we're angry, our face is ugly now, and the anger also creates the cause to be unattractive in the future. Practicing fortitude remedies this. We pray that they have magnificent qualities, that all their virtuous aspirations bear fruit, and that they benefit others.

Wishing them to have strength doesn't mean just that they have physical power or a healthy body, although those are certainly helpful. Strength includes having a strong mind, one that doesn't crumble in the face of adversity, criticism, or stress. It's a mind with clear wisdom that can remain firm and do what needs to be done with equanimity.

So often our minds are unclear and we overreact to situations. Our lack of self-esteem contributes to this, making us swirl in a tornado of indecision or drown in an ocean of confusion and anxiety. We spend so much time worrying, "I have so many things to do!" that we don't do anything. If we pause the whirlwind of anxious thoughts for even a few minutes, we will recognize that the world won't fall apart if everything on our list doesn't get done in the time frame we have planned. With a motivation of kindness, we set wise priorities we can accomplish in a reasonable amount of time. Then, with an optimistic attitude, step-by-step we do whatever is possible to accomplish them.

It sounds so easy, but why can't we do this? Due to habit, we often go into panic mode. What lies behind these habits? There's the sense of a big self. "*I* have so much to do. *I* will get blamed if it's not done. *I* will receive praise and financial reward when it's completed." But when we think about what a president or prime minister of a nation has to deal with each day, our trials and tribulations pale in comparison. I wouldn't want to be responsible for dealing with complex crises in foreign affairs that involve the life and death of thousands or millions of people. I have no stomach for political maneuvering that affects millions of people. My responsibilities are quite manageable in comparison. Seeing this, my mind becomes calmer and stronger.

We dedicate: may they find foods having hundreds of tastes and live with the food of samadhi. In the classical Indian texts, a feast with one hundred flavors was a magnificent offering to make to those worthy of honor. Here we dedicate so that our benefactors have plentiful, nourishing, and delicious food in this and all future lives. By having good health, may they lively happily and have many opportunities to create merit. May all their virtuous aspirations come to fruition.

With a good motivation, offering food to the Three Jewels, to the Sangha community, or to those who are hungry, ill, injured, or impoverished creates the cause to gain samadhi, single-pointed concentration. Meditators with deep concentration sustain their lives with the "food of samadhi." Their minds are so focused and their bodies and minds are so infused with bliss that physically, they need very little food. They are nourished physically and mentally by the power of concentration.

Tibetan meditators sometimes do the practice of *chulen*, or "taking the essence," in which they make pills with various herbs, flowers, and other substances that are consecrated with mantras. This practice is recommended only for meditators with very deep samadhi. Wanting to meditate alone without being disturbed by the need to acquire or prepare food, or by people bringing food to them, these practitioners survive only on chulen pills and water. Their meditation nourishes not only their minds but also their bodies.

I've also heard accounts of Buddhist monastics in Thailand who, last century, meditated deep in the forests where tigers and other wild creatures lived. They used the fear of dangerous animals to propel their minds into very strong states of concentration. It seemed that the forest animals sensed their virtue and didn't disturb them. When they awoke from samadhi, these meditators saw tiger footprints around them, but they were unscathed.

> By the merit of offering drink, may their afflictions, hunger, and thirst be pacified.

Here we dedicate the merit of offering drink: may the afflictions of any person who has offered us beverages of any kind—water, juice, tea, broth, and so forth—be pacified. May their ignorance, anger, attachment, jealousy, laziness, arrogance, pretension, and deceit be pacified so that they no longer create the destructive karma that brings them misery in cyclic existence and prevents them from attaining liberation.

May their hunger and thirst caused by lack of food and drink be pacified. It makes sense to dedicate that by their offering beverages their thirst would be pacified. In a more expansive meaning, "hunger" and "thirst" are often synonyms for craving in the scriptures. The mind that is hungry and thirsty craves sense objects and seeks to see beautiful things, hear enchanting sounds, smell pleasing scents, taste delicious foods, and have desirable tactile sensations. The afflictive mind could also crave a good reputation, praise, recognition, social status, and respect. The cause of our misery is not our lack of these things but the overwhelming thirst to have them. Thirst for sense objects directs many of our daily actions and drives many of our choices and decisions. When we examine our experience closely, we see that dissatisfaction and craving disturb our mental peace much more than the absence of the objects we desire.

We may think we have a lot of freedom because when we crave something we can jump in the car, go somewhere to get what we want, and satisfy that craving right away. It is possible to order almost anything in a minute online. We can quickly contact a person we want to talk to or be with. This is the common notion of freedom. Actually, when we're under the influence of strong craving, we have very little freedom; we're totally controlled by our craving. We become slaves to our desires.

Imagine what your life would be like if you weren't in a near-constant state of craving. What would it be like to feel completely content and satisfied in this very moment? Imagine feeling in the depth of your heart that who you are, what you do, and what you have is good enough. Imagine totally accepting yourself and others for who you are at this very moment. Of course, you can still try to improve in the future, but there's no hunger and thirst driving you to get something from outside — a possession, praise, sex, whatever — to validate your existence and prove that you are worthwhile. Imagine that your self-confidence is based on knowing you have the Buddha potential and that your kind heart, compassion, and generosity give you a sense of deep fulfillment.

In short, we dedicate so that our benefactors will be free from physical hunger and thirst and that the mental and emotional hunger and thirst of craving will be pacified. Although they must create the main causes for this to occur by cultivating generosity and ethical conduct and reducing self-centeredness, our prayers and dedications are cooperative conditions for the seeds of their virtuous karma to ripen.

At Sravasti Abbey, in addition to dedicating for our supporters each day, we offer the Lama Chopa *puja* and *tsok* every two weeks. At this time, we read aloud the names of all the people who have offered their resources or service to the Abbey during that half month. Once a year we do a special puja for our benefactors, posting their names on the wall of the meditation hall and reading their names aloud together with any specific prayers they would like us to make.

> May they possess good qualities such as generosity and take a rebirth without any sickness or thirst.

Generosity is one example of an excellent quality. Others are ethical conduct, fortitude, joyous effort, meditative stability, wisdom, skillful means, inner power, unshakable resolve, and pristine wisdom, as well as love, compassion, tolerance, open-mindedness, integrity, consideration for others, and forgiveness. By the virtue of others offering to us, may they have all of these good qualities and more in this and all future lives.

May they also take a rebirth without any sickness or thirst. Sickness refers to physical illnesses and injuries as well as mental illnesses. It includes being overwhelmed by afflictions—for example, when someone is sick with greed, red with anger, green with envy, or pained by a multitude of erroneous preconceptions. As before, thirst could be ordinary physical thirst as well as a mind tormented by craving, clinging, constant dissatisfaction, and emotional neediness. By virtue of their generosity in sustaining our lives, may they have physical and mental satisfaction and fulfillment in this and all their future lives.

Sealing the Offering with Wisdom

> The one who gives, the one who receives, and the generous action are not to be observed as truly existent.

By giving with impartiality, may the benefactors attain
perfection.

With this verse, we seal the benefactors' generosity with
the "circle of three." That is, we contemplate that the three —
the giver, the action of giving, and the object (the recipient
and/or the gift) — exist by mutually depending on each other.
Someone becomes a donor in dependence on there being a
recipient, a gift, and the action of giving. An object — the gift
given — becomes a gift in dependence on there being a donor,
recipient, and action of giving. The same is true for the recipient and the action of giving: none of these exist independent of the others. All of these elements are not self-enclosed
things that we stick together. Rather, their identity arises in
mutual dependence on one another. They are empty of inherent existence yet exist dependently. By means of the benefactors' generosity, done with the motivation of bodhicitta,
and sealed with the understanding of emptiness and dependent arising, may they attain the perfection of full awakening.

Not only is the benefactors' offering a generous action —
so too is our dedication of the merit created by it. We share
the merit with all sentient beings, dedicating it for the awakening of each and every sentient being. Instead of dedicating for only our own welfare, we steer the merit so it will
ripen for the well-being of all.

By contemplating the complementary natures of emptiness and dependent arising, we imbue the virtue with both
method and wisdom. Method involves the accumulation
of merit through engaging in generosity and other activities that directly benefit others. Wisdom is understanding
the ultimate nature of everything involved in these virtuous

actions. When our generosity, for example, is motivated by bodhicitta, it becomes the perfection of generosity. The perfection of generosity is far superior to ordinary generosity, which may be motivated by attachment to the recipient rather than by the expansive motivation of becoming fully awakened Buddhas so we can benefit sentient beings most effectively. When practices such as generosity, ethical conduct, and fortitude are conjoined with both bodhicitta and the wisdom realizing emptiness, they contribute to both the collection of merit and the collection of wisdom. The collection of merit primarily results in the form bodies of a Buddha, while the collection of wisdom primarily brings the truth body of a Buddha.

When we say "By giving with impartiality, may the benefactors attain perfection," "impartiality" refers to equanimity or equality, meaning that everything is equal in terms of being empty of inherent existence. This phrase reinforces our understanding that the giver, gift, action, and recipient are all equal in being empty. While they are conventionally different and perform different functions, their ultimate nature is the same in being empty of existing independently. The realization that actually cleanses all defilements and obscurations from our mind is the meditative equipoise that directly realizes emptiness and is supported by bodhicitta. Although that occurs in bodhisattvas' periods of formal meditation, we also cultivate the understanding of emptiness while doing other activities in order to integrate that understanding with our mind.

"Impartiality" also has another meaning. At the time of the Buddha, people would invite the monastics to their homes for Sangha-dana, to offer a meal to the Sangha. Householders would invite the number of monastics that they could comfortably feed, but they could not specify which of the individual monastics they would prefer to come. They would extend an invitation to the Sangha and then, according to ordination order, however many people had been requested would go for the meal. When another invitation came in, the next group of monastics in ordination order would go. This prevented favoritism. Householders couldn't specify, "We want the monastic with a good sense of humor to come because he's fun to be with," or "We want to offer to this monastic because she gives the best Dharma talks." In this way, all the monastics had a turn and were equal in sharing resources. This kind of impartiality and equality is very important for harmony in the Sangha.

Dedicating for the Benefit of All Sentient Beings

By the power of being generous, may they become Buddhas for the benefit of sentient beings, and through generosity, may all the beings who have not been liberated by previous conquerors be liberated.

In this dedication we express the wish that, by the power of being generous, all those who have made offerings to us will become Buddhas who work for the benefit of sentient beings. Whatever people may have offered to us — food, clothing, shelter, medicine, kitchen utensils, paper, vehicles, computers, seeds for the garden, tools for the forest, paintbrushes — we dedicate the merit of their generosity and the merit we create by using these offerings for the benefit of all sentient beings. Renewing our bodhicitta motivation, we pray that all of us — donors and recipients alike — quickly attain full awakening by the power of these wonderful actions of generosity.

We also dedicate for the liberation of all the beings who have not been liberated by previous conquerors. Countless conquerors — Buddhas who have conquered their afflictive and cognitive obscurations — have lived in previous eons and previous universes, but many sentient beings have not been able to meet them or hear their teachings due to lack of the virtuous karma that would bring that about. For example, Shakyamuni Buddha appeared in our world, and while many other people were able to meet him, hear teachings directly from his mouth, and immediately attain realizations including liberation, we did not. Many people met the Buddha, and although they didn't complete the entire path, they put many wonderful seeds of the Dharma on their mindstreams. These seeds will ripen in the future, enabling them to meet Dharma teachings and to practice.

We lacked the karma to meet Shakyamuni Buddha, but we had the karma to encounter his teachings now, before they fade from our world. Other beings are not as fortunate as we are. So in this verse we dedicate for all the countless sentient beings who did not meet Shakyamuni Buddha or any other Buddha so that we will attain freedom from every single unsatisfactory condition of cyclic existence. For this to come about, we must meet fully qualified teachers and have all the other conducive conditions to learn, reflect, and meditate on the Dharma. And for that to occur, we must accumulate the causes by keeping good ethical conduct, doing many virtuous deeds with compassion, and dedicating the merit for that purpose.

In this dedication verse, we direct our merit to ripen so that all of this comes about without hindrances or obstacles. May all the beings who, like us, lacked the fortune to hear the teachings directly from the Buddha, create the causes for this to happen and may we have all the external and internal conducive circumstances to study and practice the Buddha's teachings, attain liberation and full awakening, and share the healing and soothing Dharma teachings widely with others.

> By the merit of this generosity, may the *naga* kings, gods having faith in the Dharma, leaders who support religious freedom, benefactors, and others living in the area live long, enjoy good health and prosperity, and attain lasting happiness.

This verse is a broad and inclusive dedication for the present and future happiness of all sentient beings. Whether we're religious or not, everyone eats food; food is probably the item we human beings share with one another the most. Eating brings a family together; it is an activity we do socially with friends. When tragedy strikes after a natural disaster or in the wake of warfare, food is one of the first items relief agencies send in. When we are unsure how the homeless will use monetary offerings, we can give them food. Food is the universal gift that expresses care in all cultures.

Dedicating the merit of offering food reminds me that having sufficient nutritious food is a human right that is recognized in the United Nations' 1948 Universal Declaration of Human Rights (Article 25) and affirmed in the 1966 International Covenant on Economic, Social, and Cultural Rights (Article 11). Specifically, food that is sufficient in amount and quality should be available to every human being. This food should be easily accessible now and its availability sustainable in the future. No one should face discrimination of any sort or be prevented from having food.[1]

It thus makes sense to dedicate the merit we've created by offering food to the Three Jewels so that all sentient beings will benefit. We eat and drink many times each day, so offering our food and drink becomes an easy way to touch base with our spiritual values of giving and receiving kindness. It is also an opportunity to generate an understanding of dependent arising and emptiness and to create merit.

"By the merit of this generosity" refers to the generosity of the people who offered food or other requisites to the Sangha and the generosity of the monastics who offered the food to the Three Jewels before the meal.

The merit is then dedicated for various groups of living beings, some of whom we may never have heard about before. We may doubt the existence of other types of sentient beings who are imperceptible to us. Just because our senses are incapable of determining their existence doesn't mean they don't exist. For example, cats see things that we don't see. They stop suddenly and stare at a place. Sometimes they look up quickly as if tracking someone who is moving through space. Similarly, dogs will stop and listen to sounds that are beyond our auditory faculty. Perhaps they are seeing or hearing other kinds of living beings that we cannot. Nevertheless, whether we are relating to human beings, animals, insects, or any other type of living beings, our attitude should be one of loving-kindness and compassion.

Nagas are a type of sentient being found in the animal realm. Not everybody can see them, but some people report seeing naga-like creatures near streams and lakes. They have a snakelike body and tend to live in or near water, swamps, streams, marshes, at the base of trees, and so on. Nagarjuna received his name because, according to legend, he went to the land of the nagas to recover the Perfection of Wisdom sutras and bring them to the human world. The Tibetan verse dedicates for two specific naga kings, Nanda and Upananda.

Nagas are intelligent and they like their environment to be immaculate. If we dirty their living places, they express their displeasure by bringing illnesses such as skin disease. I had an interesting experience regarding this many years ago. I was doing private retreat in a cabin at a retreat center. The bathroom was quite far away from my cabin, so once in the middle of the night I thought, "Oh, there's a tree just outside; I'll pee there." The next day a gland in my neck was swollen and painful. I recited the mantra of the Buddha, the King with Power over the Nagas, and mentally apologized to the nagas for making their place dirty. Interestingly, the lump went away. Thereafter I have been more careful not to pee outdoors whenever possible in case nagas are living nearby. Nagas may live on your property, and it's important to have a good relationship with them. At the Abbey, we ask people not to pee in the forest, and every year we offer a special puja to the nagas.

Gods having faith in the Dharma are living beings in the celestial realms, particularly desire-realm gods — for example, devas who live in the forest. Many of them like to listen to Dharma teachings. Just before giving a Dharma talk, teachers often recite a short prayer inviting these devas to come and listen.

Sometimes there are small white dots that look like little lights in photographs. My Theravada friends say that these are devas who live in the area. Our forest at the Abbey is very peaceful; the energy there is very good. This could be because of these devas or other beings who live there. We human beings tend to think that we have dominion over all of nature, and other living beings just have to go along with what we want. But various scriptures advise us to temper our arrogance and be good stewards of the land and to be aware that we share it with other living beings. Some beings, such as animals and insects, we can see; others we cannot see but can sense their presence. When we first started the Abbey we made offerings to the devas and spirits who live on the land and told them of our intentions for the property — that we wish to become fully awakened in order to benefit all beings, including them — and said that we want to live peacefully together with them. Similarly, before we break ground for our buildings, we make special offerings to these other beings as well.

The verse lists the king among those for whom we dedicate, but since many of us have the fortune to live in democracies, I substituted "leaders who support religious freedom." Open-minded elected and appointed government officials who welcome diversity are important for establishing policies that bring peace to a country. Every country in the world is now multicultural and is home to multiple religions, even if the government recognizes only one official religion. The United States was founded on the principle of religious freedom and it is extremely important to protect that right in this day and age when so many people are fearful of others who are different from them in any way. The lack of religious freedom in some countries brings great suffering to residents there. In some places people are persecuted for their religious beliefs. In other places prejudice and bigotry are subtler but just as painful. Although the verse specifies leaders who support religious freedom, it implies leaders who support diversity and the well-being of all beings and who promote respect and consideration for others.

"Benefactors" refers to the people who make offerings and help us. Everyone has benefactors; we live in an interdependent world where to stay alive we need to help one another. In a family, you would dedicate for your parents, relatives, or guardians who brought you up. All of us should dedicate for the well-being of our teachers, from kindergarten on up, and for friends who encourage and support us. And some compassion and good wishes for your boss or employees, and your colleagues, would change the work environment.

Regarding the Abbey, some of our benefactors help monetarily, others come to the Abbey and work in the forest, veggie garden, or flower garden. Some are tutors for SAFE classes — our online Sravasti Abbey Friends Education courses — others help with the website, design flyers, arrange talks in other venues, and so on. Our volunteers are very precious, and we appreciate their help very much. They, in turn, benefit; we get letters and emails from volunteers all over the world who tell us how meaningful it is for them to be connected to the Abbey and how much they appreciate the opportunity to offer service, goods, monetary donations, and their prayers and dedications.

"Others living in the area" include all beings in need, as well as our neighbors, extended community, everyone residing in the country and on the planet, and all sentient beings in the universe. In the case of the Abbey, we are located in a politically conservative part of the country. Even though we may have different philosophical or political views, when it comes to kindness and consideration on a human level, we have good relationships with people in our community. To integrate with the local community, we follow the regulations set by the building, fire, and health departments. When the linemen from the public utilities department worked during a snowstorm to restore our electricity, we showed our appreciation by bringing them snacks. One day we invited the sheriff and some deputies to come for lunch, and enjoyed meeting and discussing with them. In addition to helping Youth Emergency Services, we join in local activities such as the Walk against Child Abuse and Poor People's Campaign. When the Christmas tree for the White House was taken from a nearby forest, we went to Newport to see it and chanted verses and mantras to bless it. It's suitable, proper, and respectful to dedicate for our neighbors' welfare because we share the town with them; we share the air, the roads, and water with them. We depend on each other.

Everyone wants good health and a long life, so we dedicate that all beings live long, enjoy good health and prosperity, and attain lasting happiness. May they be free of illnesses and injuries. Implicit in praying for others to have a long life is the wish that they use their longevity to create virtue through being kind and compassionate toward others.

Material prosperity is especially important for people with whom we share the planet. When welfare and resources are evenly distributed, there is less social unrest and more contentment and peace. Equal distribution of wealth frees people from jealousy and societal conflict. May everyone prosper materially and delight in sharing their wealth. May all beings experience mental satisfaction and self-respect. May they live in a wholesome way and be free from regret.

"Lasting happiness" is the happiness of full awakening. May all sentient beings be free from all the aggravating conditions of cyclic existence. May they attain liberation and full awakening. May we benefit them in this life as much as we can to repay their kindness. By the power of our practice in this life, may we progress on the path so that when we meet them again in future lives, we can teach them the Dharma and lead them on the path to full awakening. Here we consciously create a karmic link with all those who have sustained our lives or benefited us directly in one way or another. This will enable us to be of greater benefit to them in future lives. If we don't dedicate for their benefit and create that karmic connection, we may gain knowledge and realizations of the path but will be unable to share it with many people, which would be a great loss. Sharing the Dharma gives great satisfaction to bodhisattvas. For that reason, it's important to create those connections now. I see my teachers do this in many ways with all sorts of living beings. One of my spiritual mentors stops and says prayers over animals killed on the road, another puts his mala in the mouths of sea anemones at the beach.

> Due to this virtue, may all beings complete the collections of merit and wisdom. May they attain the two Buddha bodies resulting from merit and wisdom.

This verse is a well-known dedication found in Nagarjuna's *Sixty Stanzas of Reasoning*. Practitioners on the bodhisattva path put energy into fulfilling the two collections of merit and wisdom. The collection of merit—the practices of generosity, ethical conduct, fortitude, and so forth motivated by bodhicitta and done with joyous effort—pertains to the method side of the path. It is the principal cause for a Buddha's form bodies: the enjoyment body—the form a Buddha appears in to teach arya bodhisattvas in a pure land—and the emanation bodies, which are the forms a Buddha appears in to communicate with us ordinary beings. Shakyamuni Buddha is an example of the latter.

To become a Buddha a great collection of merit is not sufficient—we must also fulfill the collection of wisdom by gaining the right view of emptiness and then meditating on it for a long time in order to cleanse the defilements from our mind. The collection of wisdom is the principal cause for a Buddha's truth body, which is of two types: the wisdom truth body, which is the omniscient mind of a Buddha, and the nature truth body, which is the nonabiding nirvana and the emptiness of inherent existence of that mind.

Explained from another perspective, awakening entails understanding the two truths, which encompass all existence. Conventional truths include everything except emptiness—sentient beings, objects we use on a daily basis, virtuous and nonvirtuous actions, and so forth. We work with these skillfully to fulfill the collection of merit. Ultimate truth is the mode of existence of all these phenomena, the emptiness of inherent existence. The wisdom realizing emptiness removes all defilements from our mindstream and fulfills the collection of wisdom.

Scriptures often speak of the basis, the path, and the result. The basis includes the two truths: conventional truths and ultimate truths. The path is the method and wisdom aspects of the path. The method aspect of the path focuses on conventional truths and the collection of merit; the wisdom aspect of the path concerns the wisdom realizing emptiness and the collection of wisdom. The result is the form bodies and truth body of a Buddha. These relationships are shown in the chart below.

	Method aspect	Wisdom aspect
Basis	Conventional truths: everything other than emptiness	Ultimate truth: emptiness
Path	Activities motivated by the aspiration to be free of cyclic existence and by bodhicitta; the collection of merit	Wisdom realizing emptiness; the collection of wisdom
Result	Form body of a Buddha — Enjoyment body — Emanation body	Truth body of a Buddha — Wisdom truth body — Nature truth body

With this dedication verse, Nagarjuna brings in all aspects of the basis, path, and result and dedicates the collections of merit and wisdom so that sentient beings may attain the two Buddha bodies.

8

Eating in Moderation with Self-Acceptance

MOST OF US have some attachment to food or at least to certain kinds of food. With the exception of people who have eating disorders, this is not the most harmful type of attachment—attachment to money or to people usually gets us involved in more destructive actions. Nevertheless, it is beneficial for us to learn how to moderate and eventually release our attachment to food.

Attachment is based on exaggerating the good qualities of an object. The food on our plate looks so delicious and we crave to taste it. But if we leave it on the plate for just a little while so that it grows cold and flies land on it, it is no longer so appetizing. Along the same line, imagine what the food looks like traveling through our digestive system. We already know what it looks like when it comes out the other end. If the food were inherently tasty and desirable, it should continue to be so as it passes through our stomach and intestines. But that is not the case at all!

In addition, most of what we eat comes from dirt in one way or another. We certainly wouldn't eat a handful of dirt from the garden, yet that's where vegetables, fruits, and grains come from. Both the cause of food—the earth—and the result of food—our excrement—are not appetizing, but in the middle between the cause of the food and the effect of the food, it appears to be inherently delicious and pure. Certainly something that is caused by dirt and becomes filth is nothing to be attached to. Thinking in this way helps to reduce our exaggeration of food's desirability and our fallacious assumption that food has happiness in it, such that when we eat it, we receive that happiness.

Reciting and contemplating the verses for offering our food to the Three Jewels also helps to decrease our attachment. Since we have offered the food to the Three Jewels, it isn't very appropriate to crave what belongs to them. Accruing the karma of coveting the Buddha's possessions would not be at all advantageous for our well-being. When we offer a gift to someone, it no longer belongs to us.

The question then arises: since we offered the food to the Three Jewels, how can we eat it when it now belongs to them? There are different ways to respond to this. If we visualize the Buddha at our hearts and offer each mouthful of food to the Buddha, there is no problem. Tantric practitioners visualize themselves as the deity and offer the food to that deity. That is also fine. When we offer food on the altar, it is removed after a day or two and distributed to people to eat. Here we think that the Buddha gives us the food, and we consume it respectfully, eat it without craving, and then use the energy we receive from eating to cultivate virtuous mental states and interact with others with kindness, as the Buddha would wish.

People who are new to the Dharma easily see their attachment to food and sometimes get upset with themselves for having this attachment. They adopt an attitude of extreme asceticism, thinking they should not eat anything because they have so much attachment to food. Such an attitude is not healthy. We need to relax. Our attachment to food is mild compared to attachment to money, social status, sex, reputation, romantic relationships, praise, and approval. Also, in a place where food is easy to obtain, attachment to food doesn't inspire the intensity and type of destructive behavior that these other forms of attachment do.

At one of our annual Western Buddhist Monastic Gatherings, we were discussing how to train our mind and reduce strong afflictions. A Theravada monk explained that when he lived in Thailand, people offered beautiful meals to the Sangha, and he took a special liking to mangoes. Strong attachment to having his daily mango erupted, and he worked very hard applying all the antidotes he could think of to overcome this craving.

I gave the next presentation: "If working on my attachment to mangoes was the biggest thing I had to do in my early years of training, I would have been delighted. Instead, my teacher sent me to a Dharma center to be the disciplinarian of a group of macho Italian monks." In my work as their disciplinarian, my attachment to praise, approval, and kind words became evident because I was continuously faced with the men's blame, disapproval, and ridicule. Due to my attachment to praise and my anger at blame, I created a great deal of destructive karma, and the disharmony between a few of the monks and me adversely affected others at the Dharma center.

It's much more productive to focus on applying antidotes to afflictions that motivate highly destructive actions than to fret when attachment arises to a piece of cheese or chocolate.

This doesn't mean it's fine to always give in to that attachment. Rather, it is wiser to first emphasize cultivation of the remedies for the afflictions that cause the most harm in our lives, and slowly, gently work on attachment to food. Not eating because we hate ourselves for being attached to food does not counteract attachment to it. It is more effective to eat moderate amounts and cultivate self-acceptance.

9

Buddhist Precepts and Customs regarding Food

THE BUDDHA did not advocate harsh ascetic practices; in fact, he prohibited them. As a bodhisattva, he had engaged in ascetic practices for six years while meditating with his five companions on the banks of the Nairanjana River near Bodhgaya, India. He became so thin that when he touched his navel he could feel his spine. When the body is emaciated, the clarity of the mind is adversely affected. From his own experience, he learned that torturing the body does not subdue attachment to it. Relinquishing these severe austerities, he began to eat again. He crossed the river, sat under the bodhi tree in Bodhgaya, and overcoming all remaining afflictions, he attained full awakening.

The Buddha advocated some form of discipline when eating. For example, monastics and *anagarikas* (eight-precept holders) have the precept not to eat in the time between midday of one day and dawn of the next. Some monastics follow this precept quite strictly; others observe the meaning of the precept, which entails understanding the circumstances around which the Buddha established it.

According to the Mulasarvastivadin Vinaya followed by the Tibetan Buddhist tradition and the Dharmaguptaka Vinaya followed in China, Taiwan, Korea, and most of Vietnam, there are exceptions to the rule of not eating solid food after midday. Eating is allowed in circumstances when monastics are ill, traveling, doing manual labor, or caught in inclement weather. These exceptions are practical and emphasize the importance of not letting our health suffer by abstaining from taking food after noon. This is especially important since many monastics in India fall ill due to poor sanitation. Good health is a big aid to Dharma practice, so we should do our best to maintain it.

As mentioned earlier, at the Buddha's time all renunciates, including the Buddha's Sangha, were alms mendicants. They entered a village, going from house to house, standing silently. If a family offered food, it was gratefully accepted. If not, they went to the next house. Gathering alms differs from begging in that renunciates do not ask for food or cajole people to give them food.

Being dependent on alms, monastics had to be attentive to their practice as well as considerate of the lay people. If they were to go into the village on alms round three times a day, much of the day would be spent on this, leaving little time to meditate. If they were to eat a large or rich meal in the evening, their bodies and minds would become dull, impeding meditation in the evening and the next morning. In addition, the lay people would be inconvenienced, because they would cook multiple meals for the monastics.

Going into a village in the evening also involved some danger, as one monk unfortunately discovered. Villages at that time lacked proper toilets; people usually did their business in a field. There were no streetlights at that time, so this monk couldn't see where he was going and slipped and fell in a pit of excrement. In another incident, when monastics arrived at the door of a family after dark, the family members were frightened by strange figures appearing out of nowhere at their house, and they sometimes mistook monastics for ghosts.

With these considerations in mind, it made sense for the Buddha to establish a precept restricting the time during which monastics could eat. This worked quite well at the time, as the local food was very nourishing and the climate was moderate, so not eating after midday did not adversely affect people's health or energy level.

The Buddha allowed monastics to eat meat in most situations; this is part of the practice of accepting whatever was offered without being picky or demanding. But monastics are not permitted to eat meat in situations such as when they have killed the animal themselves, they have asked someone else to kill it, or they know that it has been killed specifically for their consumption.

When Buddhism spread to new locales, with their different climates, cultures, food, and living situations, the way food was regulated was modified. For example, when Buddhism spread to China in the first century C.E., people misunderstood the practice of going on alms round and thought the monastics were begging. This caused the Chinese to disparage Buddhism, which hindered their receptivity to the Dharma. In addition, the Mahayana tradition, which emphasizes love and compassion for all sentient beings, became prominent in China, and all monastics became vegetarian. Some people felt weak in the evening and began to have "medicine meal" in order to maintain their health and not be distracted by hunger in the evening. In Chinese temples, they usually do not chant the food offering verses before medicine meal because the food is regarded as medicine to sustain their bodies and health so that they can practice.

At the Buddha's time, monastics were not allowed to farm, because that was very time-consuming and led to their involvement in buying and selling. In addition, there was danger of killing insects. In China, monastics who resided near towns and cities were often drawn into local politics and governmental issues. Since this impeded their Dharma practice, many monastics, especially from the Chan (Zen) tradition, moved to the mountains to practice in a more secluded, peaceful ambience. Living too far from towns for people to consistently bring food to the monasteries, they began to grow their own food as part of their Dharma practice, and the precept arose, "One day without work is one day without food."

Because of the altitude and climate in Tibet, fruits and vegetables were not readily available. The Tibetan diet consisted mostly of dried meat, dairy products, and *tsampa* (ground barley flour). Since 1959, after thousands of Tibetan monastics became refugees in India, His Holiness the Dalai Lama and others have strongly encouraged reduction in the amount of meat consumed in monasteries, in favor of serving fruits and vegetables. Currently monastics don't eat meat in the large monasteries, yet many do when they eat outside. His Holiness has also advised that meat not be served during potluck meals and lunches during Dharma functions in the West.

Today in Western countries, most monastics no longer go on alms round, although some of our Theravadin friends do that from time to time. To ensure that they receive food, they sometimes tell their supporters the day and route they will take in the town. I know a small group of Theravada monks who have cultivated a warm relationship with the townspeople, most of whom are not Buddhist. These people regularly offer food when the monks go on alms round in their small town.

Some of our Zen friends who are monastics and observe the precept of celibacy do that, too. They distribute a flyer so that businesses and householders in the area know that they will go on alms round on a certain day. They ring a bell as they walk so that people who want to offer know they are there. I once went with them on alms round in Portland, Oregon. The focus was not to receive food to eat that day but to gather groceries in general. Some people came out with cooked food, but most offered groceries. The temple's lay followers walked behind us, and when our alms bowls became full, they put the offerings in large plastic bags to take back to the monastery.

Alms round is a nice tradition to keep, although nowadays it requires some planning. If we actually collected alms as they did in ancient India, we wouldn't ring a bell or notify supporters beforehand — we would simply walk quietly through town. But if we did that here, it's likely that we would go hungry, and business owners might not like monastics blocking the sidewalk.

It is up to each individual to assess the amount of food his or her body needs, and based on that decide how they will keep the precepts regarding food. When a person first ordains, it is good to keep the precepts as strictly as possible and to have only liquids after noon. If at some point you have health difficulties, then consult with your teacher about making adjustments so that you can keep the purpose and spirit of the precept, although you may not be able to keep it literally.

In any case, we must cultivate awareness of what is hunger and what is eating out of habit—either a physical or mental habit of eating. We must observe: When are we nourishing the body in order to practice the Dharma, and when are we indulging with attachment? We must also watch our mind for signs of arrogance—for instance, feeling superior because we don't eat in the evening—or signs of entitlement—such as thinking that because we don't eat after noon, we should receive large quantities of especially good food at lunchtime. One purpose of this precept is to develop within us the feeling of contentment.

The Vinaya contains many other precepts regarding food and eating. Some regard etiquette, such as not chewing with our mouth open, smacking our lips, or speaking with our mouth full. We are also to avoid looking around the room while eating to see what others are doing and to avoid looking in others' bowls to see how much food they have. Although literally this precept concerns good manners, it actually is an injunction against being a busybody who wants to know what everyone else is doing and what they have. We don't just look in their bowls but we eavesdrop in their conversations and track all the gossip about people in the various groups we belong to. This precept is an instruction to pay attention to our own bowl—our own thoughts, words, and deeds—instead of distracting ourselves by judging and having opinions about others' lives and activities.

In general we wash our own bowl afterward, although juniors often wash the bowls of those senior to them. We are also instructed to treat our alms bowl respectfully and to care for it so that it is not broken.

As mentioned in chapter 1, for lay practitioners, there is the practice of taking eight precepts for one day. In the Theravada tradition this is a type of *pratimoksha* ordination, taken with the aspiration to be free of cyclic existence. The Mahayana tradition has a practice that is similar in consisting of eight precepts, but different in that the precepts are taken with the motivation of bodhicitta that seeks to attain full awakening for the benefit of all sentient beings rather than the motivation that seeks our own liberation. In both traditions, the precepts are to avoid killing, stealing, sexual relationships (for one day), lying, taking intoxicants, sitting on high or expensive seats or beds, eating at improper times (after midday), and wearing perfumes, cosmetics, and ornaments, and singing, dancing, and playing music. While monastics may not take the eight pratimoksha precepts because they already have monastic precepts, they may take the eight Mahayana precepts because of their special motivation of bodhicitta.

Sometimes we do the Nyung Ne, or "abiding in the fast," retreat. Nyung Ne involves taking the eight Mahayana precepts for two consecutive days, eating one meal on the first day, and not eating, drinking, or speaking on the second day. The fast is broken on the morning of the third day. The real fast is abstaining from ignorance, anger, attachment, and self-centeredness. During the two days of the retreat, we meditate on Thousand-Armed Chenrezig (Avalokiteshvara) by doing many prostrations and mantra recitations, as well as practicing serenity (*shamatha*) and meditating on emptiness.

Some Buddhists choose to go on a juice fast or another type of fast, but that is something they do as individuals that is aside from Buddhist practice. The emphasis of Buddhist practice is on transforming our mind by overcoming afflictive mental states and the self-centered attitude.

10

Healing Our Dis-ease about Food

MANY PEOPLE are uneasy talking about or even thinking about their habits regarding food. In this chapter, two members of Sravasti Abbey's extended community share their experiences and thoughts about food. Bob Wilson is a longtime practitioner who is a dietician and who had his own struggles with food as a youth. Heather Duchscher is an enthusiastic Dharma practitioner who used to suffer from an eating disorder. To conclude the chapter, Dianne Pratt (a.k.a. Ven. Thubten Jigme), who was a nurse practitioner before she ordained as a nun at the Abbey, shares suggestions about healthy eating habits.

Bob Wilson: Healing the Body, Mind, and World

At certain points in my journey of life it's been very challenging to be kind and loving to the being who lives inside my own skin. I've also seen that many family members have struggled with achieving and maintaining healthy choices in their lives. These internal battles caused immense suffering for them personally, as well as for others in my family.

My heart was saddened by their distress, and I grieved that I couldn't do anything about it.

In the eighth grade, I weighed 400 pounds. Finally, at age twenty-one I said, "Holy petunias! I've got to do something!" That's when I lost over 240 pounds. I'm now sixty-six years old and have maintained that weight loss for over forty years.

That was the easy part. My mind was a mess. I had a deep need for a spiritual belief and guiding system in my life, and had tried numerous spiritual practices, but none had answered my deepest quandaries. That's when I prayed to Life, "Please help. I don't know what I need, but I need help." That's when I met Ven. Thubten Chodron and the Dharma, and this has been the most miraculous piece of my life. The teachings on mind training and the stages of the path to awakening (*lamrim* in Tibetan) provided a way for me to understand my life as well as my motivations and actions.

Early on I started going for counseling to explore how to create healthy relationships — I had never seen a healthy relationship in my extended family and wondered if they even existed on this planet. And if they did, what are their characteristics? Fortunately, my virtuous karma ripened and I met wonderful teachers such as Ven. Chodron, whose gifts and hard work for the world I deeply appreciate. Those teachers have helped me heal the wounds that my dear and precious family had never been able to heal.

I've been in a relationship for twenty years now. We've never had a fight in that time. This doesn't mean that we always agree with each other, but when we notice that one of us is invested in a certain position and cannot see things the way the other sees it, we're able to communicate about it using the nonviolent communication approach developed by

Marshall Rosenberg. We don't have to scream at each other, throw things, or slam the door and run out of the room.

We also have a common view about food, and we make healthy food choices, eating a lot of fresh food. We don't bring any junk food into the house at all. Eating healthy food has completely transformed my life.

The Buddha's teachings have also had a profound impact on my professional life. For the last twenty-six years I have taught health education, advising between twenty and sixty people every week. I asked Ven. Chodron if I could rewrite many of the meditations on the stages of the path and mind training to make them applicable for non-Buddhists. For example, the Buddha emphasized that all living beings are interconnected and interdependent. We depend on one another simply to stay alive and we continually receive kindness from others, even from strangers and people we don't always get along with. After putting some Buddhist concepts and guided meditations into secular language, I posted them on my website to help people blend healthy living with these helpful concepts. In 2009 I published the book *Lighter and Free from the Inside Out*.[1]

I know from personal experience and from working with thousands of people over the years that these Dharma principles are effective in helping people change their lives. We become what we think. We also become what we eat and what we do. Our moment-by-moment choices shape our entire life. This is the Buddhist notion of karma—our actions influence who we are and what we experience.

Applying these ideas to my own life, I was automatically able to maintain normal weight when I listened to my inner wise self to guide my choices and actions. It became evident to me that if we say we love our family and friends but do not take care of ourselves, we're out of sync. Our friends and loved ones are directly affected by our unhealthy thinking and our illnesses. It's hard for them to bear seeing us ill. If we want to show our dear ones love, we must take care of our own physical, mental, and spiritual health.

After twenty-six years of teaching about healthy living, I retired with 750 hours of sick leave to spare. Regularly making healthy food choices was a great gift. Three days a week my spouse and I go to the gym to do strength training, and we offer it up as part of our spiritual practice. For me, exercising at the gym is as exciting as watching paint dry, so I try to transform it into a spiritual practice. I say mantra and do Buddhist visualization practices while exercising. I imagine sending healing energy to everyone who is sick or injured. I pray for the other people at the gym who are struggling in their lives and trying to keep their bodies relatively healthy.

Similarly, at the grocery store, I mentally offer all the food there to all living beings, especially those who lack food and those who are ill. I also imagine the sky filled with delicious food and mentally offer it to the Buddhas and bodhisattvas. I dedicate the merit and pray for the well-being of the other shoppers around me.

I do a regular daily meditation practice, taking time to contemplate, generate compassion, and send prayers and healing energy to everybody. This little practice has changed my life; I haven't missed a day in forty-three years, and the quality of my life has improved dramatically now that I make an effort to follow Dharma principles. We never know what karmic seeds from the past will ripen, so we must continue to practice.

My urge to compulsively overeat has been completely transformed and has not returned in forty-three years. My urge to drink alcohol and take drugs has evaporated and hasn't come back in twenty-eight years. This is due to living according to the Dharma principles that the Buddha taught and Ven. Chodron has passed on to us. With her guidance and support, my life is going in a good direction.

The Abbey's motto, "Creating peace in a chaotic world," is a phrase that came to me during one of the early meetings of Friends of Sravasti Abbey. I'm happy to have contributed that. As we choose to eat healthily, generate compassion, and pray for the healing of all those who struggle with their own emotional and physical distress, we plant seeds for healing in the world and in our own lives.

Heather Duchscher: Recognizing Our Inner Beauty

In our discussion about how we relate to food and eating as Dharma practitioners, I would like to offer my personal perspective on how the Dharma has influenced my relationship with food.

I was a pretty normal kid growing up in the 1970s. I was never overweight, but I was terrified of gaining any weight whatsoever. By the time I was twelve, I was pretty heavy into dieting, and at fifteen I was anorexic. Then later on in my teens, I became bulimic. I spent about two decades teetering back and forth between starving myself (anorexia) and binging, panicking, vomiting, and then throwing out all the food in the house (bulimia). Although ostensibly I was trying to control my weight and what I was eating, actually I was seeking love and trying to control what other people thought about me so that I would feel good about myself. Obviously, food was a central part of this.

What we think about translates into our words and actions. In those twenty years of suffering from eating disorders, I did a lot of harm because of the pain I was experiencing and the way I was reacting to it with jealousy, anger, and craving. These emotions, in turn, brought more mental pain. By the time I was in my early thirties I was physically ill and mentally depressed. I had pushed my family away, and my second marriage was headed for divorce. My life was crumbling, and I was immersed in despair and hopelessness.

I was still struggling with the eating disorder, and yet I didn't know how to be any other way. I had done this for as long as I could remember. It was the way I coped with my feelings, the way I dealt with stress. It was something I did every day to some extent. I hated it and hated myself for doing it, but I didn't know any other way to be.

I met the Dharma when I was thirty-three and immediately connected with what the Buddha taught. Of course, reading a book isn't a magic wand that makes everything change overnight. Transforming our mind requires work and takes time. I was still struggling with my relationships and the eating disorder, but I was gobbling up all the Dharma books I could find. The public library had a few books on Buddhism that I read repeatedly. I found some podcasts online and listened to them over and over again.

Despite the fact that my relationships were still messy,

and I was still struggling with the eating disorder, something was beginning to change inside me. I could feel it. There was a little less attachment, a little less aversion, a little less jealousy. My mind was calming down, and I felt less despair. I found that my self-esteem was tethered less to food and eating. My sense of self-worth depended less on what I looked like and whether people liked me, and more on the potential that the Buddha says we all have for change, the potential to eliminate all our suffering and develop all good qualities.

When I first met the Dharma, I was so miserable that all I wanted was a moment's happiness. So I wasn't really paying attention to the religious side of it. I just wanted a little bit of peace because I was so unhappy.

For three or four years I read books and watched podcasts. I didn't know a single Dharma practitioner and didn't go to any Dharma centers. Then, in very rapid succession, five of my loved ones died. Life throws these things at you; it's part of being alive. One of those deaths was particularly devastating, and I was suffering a lot from the loss. All I could think about was how much time I had wasted—how much I had been consumed with counting calories and what I looked like, how much I had worried about being thin and being loved—and in the end these things didn't matter. These loved ones were gone, and I could have spent that time loving them, caring for them, being with them. I couldn't get that time back. It was gone.

I didn't want to live like that anymore. I didn't want to be controlled by food, by what people thought about me, by how thin I was. Again, progress is not like waving a magic wand. It would have been really easy to fall back into despair at that point, to retreat back into those bad habits, into harming myself and lashing out at other people due to the pain and loss. But by that time I knew enough Dharma to know that there was a way out of suffering and that I just needed to practice it to achieve the peace I sought. I knew at that point that I had to get serious about spiritual practice and that meant finding a teacher. I had no idea what that meant or how to go about it, but I knew it was important.

It took some time. Eventually I found the Bodhisattva's Breakfast Corner online (https://www.youtube.com/user /sravastiabbey), started taking the Sravasti Abbey Friends Education (SAFE) courses, and visited the Abbey. This is when things really took off. In the first SAFE course, I learned how to identify the afflictions in my mind, how to apply the antidotes right there in the moment, and how to create space between what I was experiencing and how I responded. That gave me the in-the-moment tools that I needed to work with my mind and to start healing myself and my relationships. I've now spent years doing this, and it's made an incredible difference. My identity is no longer wrapped up in food or tethered to what I look like. Rather, I focus on this beautiful potential that we have, not only to transform our own minds but also to create an environment for other people to transform theirs, too.

In short, the Dharma has given me the tools to work with my mind right in the moment—one day, one meal, one breath at a time. Practicing what I have learned has made a huge difference in my life. I hope my experience will be helpful for people who are struggling with the same issues or who know somebody who is. May the Dharma transform your mind and bring you peace and joy, as it has for me.

Dianne Pratt, NP: Eating Behaviors and Food Choice

Eating behavior and food choice are extremely complicated. The study of eating covers a range of areas from choices about what food to eat and concern about our weight, to eating-related problems such as obesity and eating disorders. Many professionals study and discuss eating behavior and food choice from social, biological, health, and clinical psychology perspectives. These people include dieticians, nutritionists, endocrinologists, geneticists, psychiatrists, sociologists, and a range of psychologists

People in all of these disciplines have developed theories about food choice in an attempt to understand why people eat what they eat and how they can be encouraged to eat more healthily. We can understand food choice on a continuum from healthy eating, to concern about our weight, to obesity and eating disorders. Studying diet entails placing our eating behavior within its social context. Although the studies and theories on diet are often explored by different researchers and published in different genres of publications, many common themes and ideas in the literature relate to gender, conflict, control, biology, communication, social norms, family, and cognition

A developmental perspective, a focus on cognition, and a psychophysiological approach are central to understanding the complexity of food choice. However, these theoretical frameworks, with their focus on the individual, minimize the complex meanings attributed to food and body shape and size. What we choose to eat is influenced by the meanings different groups of people attribute to various foods, meals as a social and cultural experience, the societal importance of being thin, and the stigma attached to being overweight. Developmental models discuss these in terms of what we learn about food by being with our family and observing others in society in general. Cognitive models address these factors by looking at social and moral norms. Psychophysiological perspectives predominantly focus on the individual's physiological makeup and how what we eat affects our body. While they can be helpful, most of these theoretical frameworks are limited and narrow in their focus. Eating behavior and food choice is a dependent arising, and there are countless causes and conditions that influence these behaviors.

Attempts to eat a healthy diet are complicated by the meanings associated with food and body size, which can result in concern about our weight. For many people, concern about weight takes the form of being dissatisfied with our body, which contributes to lower self-esteem and results in dieting and attempts to eat less. Dissatisfaction with our body can mean having a distorted body image, having a mistaken notion of the ideal body size and believing our body doesn't fit that, or simply having negative feelings about our body. At first researchers believed that dissatisfaction with our body was a problem for those with eating disorders. Now they recognize it is a common phenomenon that exists in many different groups in society.

Many dieters end up overeating and experience mild depression and a preoccupation with food. In some cases, obesity is linked to a genetic tendency to gain weight, but it is also associated with activity levels and food intake. In those individuals with a genetic predisposition for obesity, these episodes of overeating may result in weight gain, which, over many years, can result in obesity. Returning to normal weight involves changing our eating behavior, which is also linked to eating disorders such as anorexia and bulimia.

Anorexia is characterized by weight loss and is associated with a high mortality rate and a range of psychological and physical problems. Most anorexics receive help in some form or another, as the problem is easily recognized due to the loss of weight. Bulimia is more common than anorexia, although how common is unclear since many bulimics remain unrecognized — the behavior can be carried out in private and may not result in any observable physical changes. Bulimia is also associated with a range of psychological and physical problems, although the mortality rate is lower than for anorexia.

Many theories describe the causes of eating disorders, and they vary in their emphasis. Physiological models focus on the role of genetics. Other models — such as a family-systems approach, cognitive behavioral approach, socio-cultural model, and a significant-life-events model — place the individual within his or her social context. For a family-systems approach, the most important context is the family, whereas for other psychological models the broader context consisting of social meanings and norms is also relevant. At present, no single comprehensive theory explains the causes of eating disorders.

Cultivating healthy eating behaviors with a mindful, balanced perspective is the most successful approach. This approach complements our Buddhist practice of the middle way. In his first discourse, the Buddha calls the noble eightfold path the middle way because it avoids all extremes in conduct and views. It is a path of moderation between the extremes of sensual indulgence and asceticism. This supports our goal of healthy eating behavior and food choice.

Most diets are deprivation diets. Unfortunately, deprivation diets don't work very well because our body, brain, and day-to-day environment fight against them. It is estimated that over 95 percent of all people who lose weight on a diet gain it back.[2] Our body's metabolism is very efficient due to millions of years of evolution. When it has an abundance of food to burn, it increases metabolism and burns calories faster. When it has less food to burn, it burns it more slowly and efficiently. This efficiency helped our ancestors survive famines. However, it does not help today's deprived dieter. If you eat too little, the body goes into conservation mode and makes it even tougher to burn off the pounds. It seems as if our bodies and brains fight against deprivation.[3]

Research has shown that adults can lose a half a pound a week without triggering a metabolism slowdown.[4] The majority of obese people gain a pound or two each year. In a classic article in *Science* focusing on obesity, Drs. James O. Hill and John C. Peters suggested that cutting only one hundred calories a day from an obese adult's diet would prevent weight gain in most of the obese in the US population.[5] Anything a person does to make this one-hundred-calorie difference will lead those who are overweight to lose weight. One could also lose weight by walking an extra two thousand steps each day (about one mile).

Dr. Leann Birch at Penn State University and Dr. Jennifer Fisher at the Baylor Medical School have identified four ways we are conditioned to relate to food as children that impact our relationship to food and our eating behavior:

1. Food as reward: "If you get an A on your test, we'll go out for ice cream."
2. Food as guilt: "Clean your plate; children are starving in China."
3. Food as punishment: "Finish your vegetables or you can't watch TV."
4. Food as comfort: "Eat this pudding, it will make you feel better."[6]

Being aware of our conditioning—especially the four above points—can help us develop a healthy, balanced meal plan while being aware of our thoughts and feelings about eating. Food is neither punishment nor reward, but if we have been conditioned to relate to food in this way, we will need to create new behavior patterns.

What is a balanced meal? Generally, half our plate should be vegetables and fruits and the other half protein and starch. Improving our eating habits is done in small steps. The most successful method over the long term is training ourselves to approach food with a specific plan of what and how much we are going to eat as well as keeping our introspective awareness active to monitor our thoughts, feelings, and behavior as we eat.

Here are some research-based mindful eating habits that are balanced and successful for those who are overweight:

- Decrease calorie intake by one hundred to two hundred calories a day so that you won't feel deprived.
- Focus on changing small behaviors that will move you from mindless overeating to healthy eating. Evaluate the snacks you eat, where and when you snack, and what you are doing when you snack.

- Design three easy, doable changes you can make without much sacrifice.
- Use a daily checklist to help keep track. Experts in modifying behavior say it takes about twenty-eight days to break an old habit and replace it with a healthy one. With a piece of paper that has a month's worth of days across the top, write your three daily one hundred-calorie decreases down the side. Every evening, check off the changes you have accomplished. This small act of accountability will help you be more mindful throughout the day.

Although eating behavior is very complex, with intention, mindfulness, and awareness we can train ourselves to find a healthy balance without approaching food from the extremes of overeating or deprivation.

NOTES

Chapter 1: Eating as Spiritual Practice

1. Followed by lay practitioners for their entire lives, these five precepts are to abandon killing, stealing, unwise and unkind sexual behavior, lying, and taking intoxicants.
2. The eight precepts are similar to the five except the third precept is celibacy. The three additional precepts are not wearing perfumes and ornaments or singing, dancing, or playing music; not sitting on high or expensive seats or beds; and not eating after midday until dawn the following day.

Chapter 3: The Main Course

1. Those with the highest class tantra empowerment do the visualization for consecrating the inner offering.
2. The Middle Way Consequence school (Prasangika Madhyamaka) defines nirvana with and without remainder differently, where the remainder is the false appearance of inherent existence.
3. If you do tantric practice, imagine being the deity and the offering goddesses emanating from your heart.

Chapter 5: Mindful Eating

1. *Vipassana* means "insight" and is a meditation technique practiced in all Buddhist traditions. In the West the term has come to refer to meditation centers who practice a type of Vipassana meditation derived from Theravada Buddhism in Thailand and Burma (Myanmar).

Chapter 7: After-Dinner Mints

1. For more information, visit the webpages of the National Economic and Social Rights Initiative (https://www.nesri .org/programs/what-is-the-human-right-to-food) and the World Hunger Education Service (http://www.worldhunger .org/right-food-basic-human-right/).

Chapter 10: Healing Our Dis-ease about Food

1. Take a look at Bob's now-expanded website, http://www .balancedweightmanagement.com/index.html. Learn the key principles of his book at http://www.balancedweight management.com/WhyTryMyApproach.htm and http:// www.balancedweightmanagement.com/Lighter%20and%20 Free%20Description%20%20Piece.pdf.

2. See Maureen T. McGuire, Rena R. Wing, Mary L. Klem, Wei Lang, and James O. Hill, "What Predicts Weight Regain in Group of Successful Weight Losers?" *Journal of Consulting and Clinical Psychology* 67, no. 2 (1999): 177–85.

3. See Roy F. Baumeister, "Yielding to Temptation: Self-Control Failure, Impulsive Purchasing, and Consumer Behavior," *Journal of Consumer Research* 28, no. 4 (2002): 670–76.

4. This conclusion is from a series of studies alluded to in David A. Levitsky, "The Non-Regulation of Food Intake in Humans: Hope for Reversing the Epidemic of Obesity," *Physiology & Behavior* 86, no. 5 (December 2005): 623–32.

5. See James O. Hill and John C. Peters, "Environmental Contributions to the Obesity Epidemic," *Science* 280, no. 5368 (May 1998): 1371–74.

6. Leann L. Birch and Jennifer O. Fisher, "Mother's Child-Feeding Practices Influence Daughters' Eating and Weight," *American Journal of Clinical Nutrition* 71 (2000): 1054–61; Leann L. Birch, Linda McPhee, B. C. Shoba, Lois Steinberg, and Ruth Krehbiel, "Clean Up Your Plate: Effects of Child Feeding Practices on the Conditioning of Meal Size," *Learning and Motivation* 18, no. 3 (1987): 301–17.

GLOSSARY

afflictions. Mental factors that disturb the tranquility of the mind. These include disturbing emotions and wrong views.

afflictive obscurations. Obscurations that mainly prevent liberation; afflictions, their seeds, and polluted karma.

arhat. Someone who has eradicated all afflictive obscurations and is liberated from samsara.

arya. Someone who has directly and nonconceptually realized the emptiness of inherent existence.

bodhicitta. A main mental consciousness induced by an aspiration to bring about others' welfare and accompanied by an aspiration to attain full awakening oneself.

bodhisattva. Someone who has spontaneous bodhicitta whenever he or she encounters a sentient being.

Buddha. A fully awakened being who has abandoned all obscurations completely and developed all excellent qualities limitlessly.

cognitive obscurations. Obscurations that mainly prevent full awakening.

collection of merit. A bodhisattva's practice of the method aspect of the path that accumulates merit.

Glossary

compassion. The wish for sentient beings to be free from all duhkha and its causes.

cyclic existence (samsara). The cycle of rebirth that occurs under the control of afflictions and karma.

Dharma. (1) The Buddha's teachings. (2) True cessations and true paths that are one of the Three Jewels.

duhkha. Unsatisfactory experiences of cyclic existence.

emptiness. The lack of inherent existence, lack of independent existence.

full awakening. Buddhahood; the state where all obscurations have been abandoned and all good qualities developed limitlessly.

ignorance. A mental factor that is obscured and grasps the opposite of what exists. There are two types: ignorance regarding reality that is the root of samsara, and ignorance regarding karma and its effects.

karma. Volitional action.

liberation. The state of freedom from cyclic existence.

Mahayana. A collection of sutras and a way of practice that emphasizes attaining full awakening in order to benefit all sentient beings.

merit. Good karma.

mind. The clear, immaterial and aware part of living beings that cognizes, experiences, thinks, feels, and so on.

monastic. Someone who has received monastic ordination; a monk or nun.

nirvana. The cessation of afflictive obscurations and the rebirth in samsara that they cause.

pratimoksha. The different sets of ethical precepts that assist in attaining liberation.

samsara. The cycle of rebirth that occurs under the control of afflictions and karma.

Sangha. (1) One of the Three Jewels that is a reliable guide on the path; (2) The monastic community consisting of four or more fully ordained monks or nuns.

sentient being (sattva). Any being with a mind that is not free from pollutants; i.e., a being who is not a Buddha. This includes ordinary beings as well as arhats and bodhisattvas.

Tathagata. A Buddha.

Theravada. The predominant form of Buddhism practiced today in Sri Lanka, Thailand, Burma, Laos, Cambodia, and so forth.

Vinaya. Monastic discipline; the scriptures that present the monastic discipline.

ABOUT THE AUTHOR
AND SRAVASTI ABBEY

BHIKSUNI THUBTEN CHODRON is an American Buddhist nun in the Tibetan tradition. Ordained in 1977, she is a student of His Holiness the Dalai Lama and other Tibetan masters. She teaches Buddhism internationally; is the author of many Dharma books, including *Buddhism for Beginners*; and is the founder and abbess of Sravasti Abbey, a Buddhist monastery in Washington State, USA, where she lives. She is active in social engagement, including teaching Dharma to incarcerated people and sitting on the board of Pend Oreille County Youth Emergency Services. See https://www.thubtenchodron.org.

Throughout the ages, monasteries have been centers of Buddhist learning and practice, places that have benefited monastics, lay practitioners, and society. Since 2003, Sravasti Abbey has continued that tradition, providing a quiet environment conducive for Buddhist study, practice, and meditation. The Abbey is a residential community of fully ordained monastics, novices, and trainees. They also welcome visiting lay and monastic practitioners who are interested in living, working, and practicing in a community setting. Please come and visit! For more information, see https://www.sravasti.org.